Toxic Mythology

Toxic Mythology

Breaking Free of Popular Lies and Cultural Poison

DOLORES T. PUTERBAUGH

RESOURCE *Publications* • Eugene, Oregon

TOXIC MYTHOLOGY
Breaking Free of Popular Lies and Cultural Poison

Copyright © 2015 Dolores T. Puterbaugh. All rights reserved. Except for brief quotations in critical publications or reviews, no part of this book may be reproduced in any manner without prior written permission from the publisher. Write: Permissions, Wipf and Stock Publishers, 199 W. 8th Ave., Suite 3, Eugene, OR 97401.

Resource Publications
An Imprint of Wipf and Stock Publishers
199 W. 8th Ave., Suite 3
Eugene, OR 97401

www.wipfandstock.com

ISBN 13: 978-1-62564-768-9
Manufactured in the U.S.A.

To my husband, Gerry. Thank you for everything.

Contents

Foreword | *ix*
Acknowledgments | *xi*
Introduction: Myths Old and New | *xiii*

1. It Runs in the Family: Hereditary, Genetics, Environment, Fate, and Free Will | 1
2. Free to Be . . . Whatever, Whenever: The Myth of Endless Options | 17
3. You Should Go Out, and Not Be So Antisocial | 34
4. Your Opinion is as Good as Anyone Else's | 46
5. Money Can't Buy Happiness, or Can It? | 60
6. That's My Personal Life: Compartmentalization | 75
7. Sticks and Stones | 92
8. Conclusion | 107

Foreword

WHEN A PSYCHOTHERAPIST DRAWS on professional experience, the client's privacy and well-being outweighs everything else. With that standard in mind, the cases presented in this book are fictional. While I have learned much from my clients and friends over the years, I am not at liberty to divulge their personal experiences in book form. My professional experience informs my writing but my writing is not a disclosure of professional experience.

Acknowledgments

THIS BOOK WOULD NOT have been possible without the help of my dear friends, Wayne Barrett and Scott Wilson.

This book has been developed in part from work published in USA Today Magazine, and I am grateful for the support and editing provided by the publisher, Wayne Barrett, over the years. I am more grateful for his friendship. Thank you, brother.

Scott is a stalwart friend, patient reviewer and tireless cheerleader. Thank you.

Introduction
Myths Old and New

TELL ME A STORY; tell me your favorite movies, your favorite books, the stories of your life, and you will tell me much more than you might have intended. The stories we tell reveal at least as much about ourselves as about the characters in the tales. Consider how your friends' interior lives are exposed through the stories they choose to share. It's not just the facts; the details, the emotional subtext, the underlying assumptions within stories, communicate our world view, hopes, dreams and fears. In family therapy, this is often referred to as the "Report and Command" function of communication. The "report" comprises the information; the "command" is the unspoken subtext.

> "My children only call me once a week now that they've moved to their own apartments," complains a parent. That's the report: it is merely the facts. The unspoken message, the command? "... But they should call more often," or, "and I want them to call more often," or perhaps, "I am hurt and angry that they do not call me more often," or, possibly at the deepest level, "I am consumed with guilt over my errors in parenting, and wonder if I am to blame for their neglect."

"Command," in this context, doesn't mean dictates. Instead, it means the implied wishes and hoped-for-actions. In the example of the complaining parent, the factual statement is, in effect, a clumsy,

Introduction

terse shorthand for the deep longing and disappointment this parent feels over the children's emotional and physical distance. Just listening to the facts tells us little, because it is the interpretation and effects of the facts that matter so much to our storyteller. Is the parent entitled to adult children who always initiate contact, or is the parent someone all too aware of past sins against these children, wondering if it is a natural and tragic comeuppance that the children have spun off into detachment?

Stories don't only tell us about the storyteller and the subject. The stories people tell us teach us how we are seen through their eyes. Communication isn't merely to relay information; it's about exchanging ideas, creating and strengthening connections, and sharing support. We tell one another about our ideas, emotions and experiences in order to achieve these ends, and we often learn quickly which stories, feelings and thoughts to share with whom. Children adapt to this, telling secrets to a best friend until betrayed, not telling parents about their crushes when puberty hits, and learning rapidly what is worth bringing forward in class discussions. Except for children still struggling to read social cues and budding narcissists, bragging about how easy something is in class is never done; offering too many right answers is a recipe for peer disapproval. Peer approval remains important, to some degree, throughout life. We want the approbation of our friends, so we choose the stories that will build positive connections. When a friend routinely shares the latest gossip about a celebrity or a mutual acquaintance, that friend is communicating to you the implicit belief that it is this sort of news that attracts and holds your attention.

Sometimes, we share to impress; young people inflate their accomplishments in person and on social media, and adults do, as well. We tell stories that are little personal legends. In doing so, we tell others more important things:

> *"I don't think I'm lovable as I am; I have to present a false self."*
>
> *"I can't trust you to accept me as I am."*

Introduction

"I believe you are the kind of superficial person who is impressed by bragging."

In other words, the friend who believes that sharing gossip about someone else's misfortune is the means to grab your undivided attention is telling you some pretty unflattering things about you. The friend who thinks you are the right person to hear tales of joy is telling you something else entirely. Of course, not all stories are personal. Sometimes we tell stories that transcend our daily lives. We use allegories, metaphors, and examples from history and art. Different levels of stories reflect different levels of understanding. A great story reveals great truths. Myths are great stories.

For this discussion it is necessary that we agree on the definition of myth. The word "myth," itself, is as much a victim of the corruption of our language as the myths addressed in later chapters. A myth, in its original sense, is a story that communicates a greater truth. Much of what we now point to as myth were ancient religions, in times and cultures in which revelation was very much in its early stages. The people of these times were attempting to make sense of the cosmos, to put into words their sense of awe and their understanding of the supernatural world. They lacked knowledge of the one God, although we know some worshipped at the temple of the Unknown God, a prescient acknowledgement that myth cannot explain everything.

Given the profound beauty and power of creation, it makes perfect sense that myths are often fantastical, full of imagery and drama. They were intended, in the days of strictly oral communication, to grab the listeners' imaginations, engage the mind and heart, creating the fertile ground for the great truth. From earliest days, humans attempted to make sense of a world that was plainly beyond explanation. We see this very clearly in the two Genesis stories of the Creation; while the early oral tradition communicated that God created everything, and attempted a summary, science was not available to support understanding. It turns out, of course, that the gradual unfolding of life forms described in Genesis correlates quite nicely to aspects of the fossil record, even if the timeline proposed by the inspired authors was a bit abbreviated. The timeline is merely a device of the myth; the essence is that God created everything and that we may attempt to understand but we will always be insufficient to that task. It is a beautiful thing then, to consider the scientific theory of the sudden creation of the known universe, the Big Bang theory, first described by Fr. Georges LeMaitre and shortly thereafter, and more famously by Hubble. *"And God said, Let there be light . . . and (bang!) there was light . . . And God saw that the light was good."* It's hard to find a better example of science supporting "myth" as a great truth, than this.

Of course, the term "myth," like "legend," and "fable," has been downgraded much in recent decades. Someone who has been a celebrity for a few years is a "legend," and a rumor about someone cooking themselves to death via substituting vegetable shortening and foil for sunscreen is shrugged off as "just a myth." This has been done so frequently that the word "myth" has become a synonym for "falsehood." When we point to myths, then, we have to scramble around the modern, shallow definitions and point to the true and historical meaning.

To make matters worse, the great truths in some of the most common and durable myths have become corrupted of late.

A telling example of an ancient myth, with its terrible truth, and its modern, corrupted version is the myth of Narcissus. He was handsome, accomplished, and self-absorbed. Depending on which version of the myth you choose, his cruelty and rejection led others to suicide or dying of heartbreak. Ultimately, his self-absorption led to his own destruction. His name is, of course, the root word of narcissism. Narcissism used to be recognized as a character disorder in psychiatry; now it has devolved into being called a mental disorder, one of many personality disorders. It sounds quite bland in the diagnostic manual; we have lost the deep tragedy of Narcissus. Seeing narcissistic behavior merely as one form of mental disorder, it is easy to lose sight of the fact that an excessive amount of self-absorption and disregard for others is destructive ultimately not just to others but to the self. The myth also relays something else: that people voluntarily gave themselves over to Narcissus. The superficial attraction and the charisma of arrogance ensnared and ultimately, destroyed them. That is a critical part of the myth, and not one that glazing over it with a "personality disorder" label adequately amplifies.

> "Joe" is wealthy, a leader in his industry, and good-looking. He exploits these factors to attract women. Many of the women he chooses are worldly and sophisticated; they "know the game," as Joe describes it, and understand that they are exchanging their companionship for temporary trappings of wealth: expensive dinners, gifts, travel in private jets. Sometimes, though, Joe is bored with women as jaded as he, and amuses himself by pursuing someone different: someone naïve, fresh and open to life. Recently, he drew in a woman close to his age, "Connie," who believed him when he said he cared about her. Connie was impressed with the hard work and intellect that created his fortune. Connie didn't understand the "game," and Joe was not touched, only mildly entertained, by her emotional pain and weeping outburst when, after unceremoniously ending their relationship, he took care to be sure he encountered her often with his latest lady-friend. Connie was crushed and humiliated; Joe was amused. As a narcissist, he was incapable of empathy and of appreciating Connie – or anyone else – as a human being.

"Joe" is a narcissist. Children who meet Narcissus through mythology, and understand him are better prepared to make sense of the befuddling, seemingly contradictory behavior of narcissists.

The idea of telling myths, to children and adults, was to share these essential truths. Unfortunately, if children are introduced to useful myths at all, it is in a rather cursory way and often the deeper meanings are brushed aside. The point of learning about Greek and Roman mythology is not just to learn the names of characters; that was not the point of cultural literacy. Understanding the meaning of those myths, and integrating that knowledge into one's understanding of human nature, was the point. When children have not reached the age of abstract thinking, they are necessarily missing part of the story.

Introduction

Until children reach around age 11 or 12, they are in what developmental psychologists call the "concrete operations" stage of mental development. Many adults stay in this stage; attaining the ability to think in very abstract terms doesn't happen for everyone. Children take things literally. They deal with the real, material world and only over a period of brain maturation, gradually move into the world of ideas and thinking about their own thinking. When children are in the concrete stage of development, they can learn the stories but the stories are only going to be the rudimentary scaffolding for deeper understanding.

For example, many children meet "Sleeping Beauty" at a young age. They hear about good and bad fairies, meek pretty girls, and bold princes who save the kingdom. It would be helpful for children to hear the whole story at a later age, when the abstract principles can be integrated into the beginnings of wisdom. The story of Sleeping Beauty tells what happens when people give free reign to jealousy and envy, and the dire outcomes when silly measures are taken to cope with risk. Banning sewing needles does not keep misfortune at bay. We won't go into the Ogress' trying to trick the prince into eating his own children and wife. Did you miss that part of the story? That's because in the past two generations, the retelling has focused on pretty girls, fancy dresses and somewhat creepy stalker behavior held up as a model of salvific masculine love. Whether that is a good myth in terms of fostering an understanding of good and evil remains to be seen.

Children learn about the Greek and Roman gods and goddesses now in largely superficial ways, or see them misrepresented as cartoon characters, and the point of the mythology is lost. It is easily morphed into a kind of sneering at how silly those ancient people were, imagining the sun was a blazing chariot or that winter comes because someone is weeping for her daughter. In such a case, re-introducing the story later, when the brain is more mature and ready for more complex thoughts, is optimal. As remarked earlier, even bright children are generally quite concrete in their thinking until around age 11 or 12. While they may begin to surmise more abstract truths, the capacity for formal logic, grasping

Introduction

deeper meanings and applying those meanings across novel situations requires a level of cortical development that only occurs gradually. The first introductions smooth the process to deep understanding when material is reintroduced.

This was the thought behind C. S. Lewis' work in The Chronicles of Narnia. It was his hope that, by reading about Aslan and the other denizens of Narnia, when his readers eventually encountered Jesus and the story of our salvation that it would seem as if they have known Him all along. The furrows and rows for that seed have been prepared and fertilized by the adventures in Narnia. In the case of Narnia we have been given a deliberately created myth intended to foreshadow a preexisting Truth. In the case of Narcissus, we have an ancient myth of varying forms, communicating an essential truth. In both cases, the message is powerful and inspires reflection and movement to make changes for the better.

We rarely teach our children the old and great myths, but our culture certainly feeds them misinformation and truisms dressed up like essential truths. They are pseudo-myths, purporting to carry some deep and powerful message to change our lives, but in reality they are misrepresentations, not myths. These modern myths sometimes contain an essential truth, but one that has been twisted. In other cases, the myths are such distant shadows of a truth that they are harmful lies. In the following chapters, we will break open some of these modern myths, explore their psychological and spiritual underpinnings, the harm in the modern message, and possibilities for corrective action if the myth has taken root.

1

It Runs in the Family
Hereditary, Genetics, Environment, Fate, and Free Will

DO YOU HAVE BLUE eyes? Blue eyes are the result of a genetic anomaly, a birth defect of sorts, originating only 10,000 years ago. That trait runs in your family. How about your penchant for debating anything under the sun? Your aversion to heat or cold, or your attraction to redheads? Do those also run in the family?

All sorts of problems, behaviors and talents run in families. Athletic ability, intelligence, temperament and various ailments all carry a sizeable slice of heritability. The 2012 Summer Olympics featured 11 sibling pairs in the various swim events, suggesting a convergence of nature and nurture. IQ is significantly correlated to parents' intelligence. Temperament, with its sizeable biological component, tends to be similar among family members, with outliers suffering the consequences. Mental and physical disorders of various stripes tend to recur across generations, too.

The myth of family heritage and the assumption of powerlessness is epidemic. "(Emotional diagnosis of concern) runs in the family," a client will explain to me, as if only the simple-minded lacked the knowledge of genetics needed to grasp this. This statement is sometimes supposed to be a blanket pass, a "get out of jail free" card against any personal responsibility to make things better. At other times, it is a plea for help: the implicit cry is, "Please, tell me I'm wrong—that I won't be schizophrenic/bipolar/crazy like my mom/dad/sibling." Indeed, many emotional struggles and unfortunate behavioral tendencies can and do "run in families," but the relationship between this, and some sort of preordained doom is often a tenuous one.

It is helpful to be certain that we agree on definitions. In my business of mental health, one thing that is painfully clear is that people throw psychiatric terms around with abandon, believing we all understand them to mean the same thing. A client complains of being "depressed" and is surprised that this one word does not tell me precisely what the client's lived experience may be. "Depressed" can be a euphemism for "furious and resentful," or it may mean that the person is dysthymic, feeling weighed down and gently morose, like a human Eeyore the Donkey. A depressed person may be suicidal. He may feel flattened, or weep for hours a day, or suffer a state of mental agitation. The 5th edition of the American Psychiatric Association's Diagnostic Manual takes more than 30 pages to go through the various criteria for numerous varieties of depression.

Similarly, when we assert that some trait, talent or trouble "runs in the family," we ought to be clear. Like "depression," everyone who uses the term "running in families" is absolutely certain that they, and their listeners, know precisely what it means. Of course, everyone does not. Something that runs in the family may be due to any single factor, or amalgamation of factors, including deliberately learned behaviors, unconsciously adopted attitudes, beliefs and patterns of thinking, the externals of culture, genetics, and numerous physical aspects of the environment.

The Behaviorist perspective on the human experience emphasizes learning. From our earliest moments on earth, we are learning. Before birth, children can recognize their mother's voices; they share the adrenaline rush and racing heart rate she

It Runs in the Family

experiences in moments of distress. Research from the Gottman Institute suggests that the child's basic temperament — calmness and receptiveness to soothing — can be predicted with great accuracy by observing the parents' style of disagreeing during the child's last three months in utero. During the first years of life, a tremendous amount of learning occurs, with the properly fed and nurtured infant building millions of neural connections on an upwards slope that will only gradually level off in preschool and the early school years, when the first major pruning of unneeded connections begins.

Children are constantly acquiring new information. Sometimes it is information we don't want them to have; sleeping infants' brain waves change when their parents are arguing quietly in another room. Eager sponges, children imitate gestures, expressions, and sounds. They mimic adult behaviors; the family full of readers, who read to the infant, and are seen sitting around reading for entertainment, will have a toddler very likely to consider books as friends, and something one takes along on outings like a toy, to occupy spare moments. Conversely, I have spoken to educators who share heartbreaking stories of kindergarten students who, when handed a book, look befuddled. They have never held a book; they do not know what it may be. These are not third-world children; they are living in homes that have televisions but no books. Their ignorance about books and the value of formal education does, indeed, "run in the family."

Children also learn to think by listening to grownups and bigger children speak. After all, what is speaking but thinking aloud? Children exposed to a lot of clear, positive and interactive speech, learn to think this way. Children whose grownups evidence an internal locus of control, encourage the child to master new skills and praise effort over outcome, especially early in the learning process of any skill, are children who are set up to have a sense of personal competence. Encouraged to take small risks, and praised for their efforts, they are comfortable struggling through the necessary missteps in the learning process. They are engaging in the world on multiple levels. Developmental theorist Jean Piaget described children at this stage as "small scientists," testing their hypotheses through active, exploratory play.

Children likewise learn from siblings, from playmates, electronic media, books and their own experiments with the environment. Sometimes it is simple imitation, as when a child finally speaks with bell-like clarity, and the first real word is the profanity a parent let slip in a moment of pain or annoyance. At other times it is a deliberate process of shaping, as when the parents first praise any effort to move food from plate to mouth, then any effort involving a rubber-coated spoon, and finally successful use of the spoon. Sometimes children choose the behavior to imitate via vicarious reinforcement; a peer is given lots of attention for some sort of behavior and thus that behavior is imitated in search of that reinforcing attention. At other times, parents and teachers inadvertently reward the wrong behaviors and the child figures out the level of misbehavior that will be tolerated. Any parent who has made the fateful error of yielding to a checkout line tantrum has learned that it can take a year of consistent resistance to tantrums to overcome that single moment of weakness. In any case, the child's actions—for better or blue-faced, screaming on the floor worse—were learned.

Similarly, a child may observe very carefully how the adults handle life's events. If bullying, getting drunk or stoned, or any other sort of inadequate coping strategy is what is used to get through difficult times, count on the child absorbing that lesson. The child may merely ape the bad behavior, or learn to expect that treatment from future loved ones. It is also possible the child will stonily resolve to do whatever is the opposite and inadvertently toss away any positive lessons from that particular role model.

Other perspectives on family traits, such as the broad field of psychodynamic theories, emphasize a different kind of learning, including introjection. Introjection is one of those wonderful Freudian terms truly rooted in the ancient philosophers. It speaks to the unconscious type of learning, by apparently effortless absorption. It is one subset of learning, and the subsequent beliefs, impressions, and psychological scaffolding are experienced directly as having always been there, as being "natural," or something "everyone knows." These are the underlying assumptions upon which children act in terms of budding morality. It is the beginnings of conscience. Conscience, of course, will later require deliberate formation, reflection and responsible seeking of knowledge—or be fated to remain at a small child's level of conscience in which good and bad are defined in the simplest, and crudest level of moral decision making: what will result in punishment or reward?

This is where we all start out, morally: we are either mimicking, or actively learning what will be rewarded or punished. Along the way, we develop some baseline empathy. Infants normally respond with distress to other children's crying and, once mobile, will often move to try to comfort. Over time, this combination of innate empathy and learned behaviors drives a toddler to rub the back of a weeping peer, saying, "It's OK." The child has learned the behavior (say encouraging words and offer a comforting touch to someone in distress) and has the internal motivation of natural empathy. Eventually the combination becomes entrenched as a behavior pattern and the child's natural tendency, plus the expectation that we comfort those in distress with a combination of words and actions, will seem to be a wholly natural sequence. Empathy, in healthy people, is a natural phenomenon. The particular means to express it are shaped by experience.

The kind of behavior that is used to express empathy and give comfort is in part cultural. Our cultural environment provides a mental scaffolding on which we organize experiences, thoughts and feelings. Empathy is not the only aspect of emotional experience subject to culture. In other words, our social milieu influences the ways in which we learn to interpret internal and external experiences, give meaning to experiences, and share those experiences with others. This social aspect to our development in terms of how we think, feel and behave, is a tremendous factor in what does, or does not, "run in the family."

Consider the issue of schizophrenia, a hot-button topic in the arena of medical vs. non-medical theories of mental illness.

Toxic Mythology

Schizophrenia, a psychiatric diagnosis in the Diagnostic and Statistical Manual of Mental Disorders (5th ed.), published in 2013 by the American Psychiatric Association, does not exist per se. It is not an "it," but rather a construct, representing the agreed-upon criteria and parameters as defined by a large committee of psychiatrists and other professionals reviewing the latest research. No educated person in the mental health field is pretending there is one "it," one specific entity comprising the etiology of all experiences labeled as schizophrenia. In other words, right now schizophrenia is diagnosed off a list of symptoms; meet enough criteria and the diagnosis is given. The diagnosis does not tell us which of the many causes may be related to the person's suffering: a virus? Drug abuse? Trauma? Brain injury? We don't know, and psychiatry does not yet have the means to medically separate the causes for similar lists of symptoms. Five patients may exhibit similar symptoms but have very different causes underlying the seemingly similar suffering.

There are multiple current theories of the causes of the same, or similar enough, sets of internal experiences and observable behaviors that fall within the diagnostics criteria of schizophrenia. One is prenatal acquisition of a viral infection that lies dormant and occasionally flares, resulting in mania and psychosis. There is substantial research on this, largely in Europe, but also performed at Johns Hopkins over 20 years ago; many patients benefitted profoundly from mega-doses of intravenous antivirals and were able to return to their normal lives with no residual effects and no need for ongoing psychiatric treatment, until the next viral flare. Another explanation is that often young adults have what would have been (and, in third world countries, often is) a single psychotic break, possibly due to a combination of factors such as stress, genetic vulnerability, poor life habits and what we now know is a critical time of brain reorganization. In societies where the young person in question can temporarily withdraw from most stressful obligations, and get physical activity, adequate rest, good nutrition, and positive social supports, the remission rate for what we call schizophrenia is quite high. The Quakers' farms for

It Runs in the Family

the mentally ill, run in the United Kingdom and the United States during the 19th century, are a very clear illustration of this practice. As far as modern international trends, I refer interested readers to the World Health Organization's report on this, in which, only 3% of US residents diagnosed with schizophrenia will have complete remission, compared to 54% of Indian residents with the same diagnosis. Something about the cultural experience of the phenomena, as well as the nature of the care given, powerfully changes the experience and its meaning. Using this example, we can see how the way the culture frames and interprets experiences sets expectations and seems to influence, if not determine, the outcome of the experience.

Another aspect of "running in the family" subsumes a complex stew of genetics, epigenetics and the environment. When speaking of genetics, we are referring ultimately back to the hard science that has its roots in Fr. Mendel's rigorous 19th century work with vegetables. Genes are the precise blueprinting information that is passed forward from parent to offspring, whether in plants or animals. Whatever appearances and behaviors may be, the split is 50/50: a child's precise genetic inheritance is no more from one parent, biologically, than the other. Some information is dominant and expresses itself in the presence of a recessive gene inherited from the other parent. The recessive gene lurks in the background but is not necessarily either silent or ineffective. Brown eyes are dominant over blue eyes, but the brown eyed-girl may have a blue eye gene hanging around to pass forward for generations before it expresses, surprisingly, in a great-grandchild. Both blond and red hair colors are recessive; the offspring of this combination are an interesting result of genetic arm-wrestling between two sets of recessive genes. Recent decades have explored so-called "junk DNA" which turns out not to be junk, after all. Like the apparently redundant organs of the Klingon warriors of Star Trek, even junk DNA can come in very handy at times. Just because someone hasn't figured it out, doesn't mean it will not ultimately make sense, or will not shed considerable light on curing cancer. DNA is hereditable.

Toxic Mythology

Heredity, though, is a slippery concept. It is so deceptively clear; like many terms, everyone supposes that everyone else means the same thing. An inheritance might be genetic, a pile of money, or a reputation in the neighborhood. When it comes to our physical nature, it turns out that we can inherit certain things that are not necessarily genetic in nature. The kind of nutrition and health, or lack of it, our grandmothers enjoyed in their reproductive years will affect the degree to which we express the full range of health that our genetic predisposition, environment and behaviors should have garnered. The stamina of Grandma's ova, therefore, ultimately was passed to her child—your parent—and then on to you. This is a fairly new trend in research which, of course, is not going to yield experiments done on humans but will no doubt combine animal experimentation with the gathering of detailed information from families where DNA confirms the line of descent. Worldwide, a good 10% of paternity is, to put it politely, "misattributed;" that is yet another blow to the notion of things "running in families," or being "hereditary."

Even when considering genetic predisposition, there is the substantial factor of diasthesis-stress. As any intro-psych student can tell you (or better be able to, by the end of the term), the interaction of life experiences with biology can lead to a wide range of outcomes. Sometimes the life experiences are within our control; a person who has high blood pressure on both sides of the family can proactively adopt a very healthy lifestyle and counteract a good deal of the risk. At other times, the circumstances are thrust upon us: victims of violent crime or natural disasters, for example. In such cases, a very sensitive, vulnerable individual, when exposed to stressors, may struggle more than a less neurologically sensitive person.

Of course, even in the brief prior paragraph, numerous sorts of "runs in families" are stirred into the soup. The person with medical problems "running in the family" may have a genetic predisposition to cardiovascular problems, or may simply be the fruit of two families with appalling lifestyles. At some point she developed an internal locus of control (learned, and therefore the

It Runs in the Family

psychic runoff of someone else or multiple someones) and believed that in the face of difficult situations she could do something to mediate the outcome. We do not know if she is over-reacting because there is no real elevated risk; if the families' tendencies towards cardiac issues are genetic, there is a heightened biological risk. If the families' misfortune is due to learned behaviors involving sitting around and infusing massive amounts of corn syrup, white bread and all the wrong fats, then our sample reactor has less biology and more culture to overcome. On the other hand, she managed to inherit, through learning, the belief that she can do something about this inheritance.

A predisposition, combined with circumstances—even circumstances where there is no option — are another mixed bag. We learn from our earliest moments of life; this, too, is a form of inheritance. Consider the new mother with post-partum depression. She is exhausted, sad, numb, and feeling guilty because she ought to be happy and she cannot rally more than a shadow of joy. Meanwhile, our modern lifestyle has deprived her of the wrap-around care of an extended family; she is alone much of the day with an infant who requires immediate, near-constant, tender attention. Our primitive ancestors would have afforded this mother more physical care, more attention, and perhaps a blood relative nursing the child from time to time so the mother could rest. The child would not have been alone with an anemic, exhausted, and discouraged parent. Depressed people are slow to respond, with flattened expressions and voices. The infant may learn important and, perhaps, indelible lessons from this mother. These may include that often crying is for naught; help for the scary pain of hunger or need for comfort does not seem to come. Attempts at connecting—cooing, reaching, gazing—likewise garner little reaction. The child develops a kind of primitive depressive mindset, due to what social scientists call "learned helplessness," the opposite of the internal locus of control. Instead of learning that her actions yield useful results, she feels that nothing she does really matter. She is not receiving the stimulation and comfort that will allow for optimal neurological, intellectual and emotional development.

Toxic Mythology

The child is being "set up" for depression. This is a very dark inheritance that needs no genetic predisposition. The same baby, with attentive aunts, older sisters, grandmothers or family friends nearby to pitch in, would get all the tender, immediate care needed to provide optimal development, and mom would have a chance at getting the recuperative rest needed to overcome the blood loss, violent hormonal swings of pregnancy and childbirth, and sleep deprivation that are part of the postpartum experience.

Science is producing a growing body of research that allows us to do something about those things that run in families in a genetic sense. The abnormalities of the BRCA-1, BRCA-2 and other genes that carry the threat of breast and ovarian cancer are one example. One hopes that that we will soon have treatments that counter the gene expression rather than the current option: the attempt to short-circuit its expression by removing vulnerable body parts. In the cases of genetically transmitted risks, it must feel very insulting to have these real, inherited, biological and presently inescapable problems that run in their families lumped in with those of people who have no such biological burden but have chosen to have poor diets, sit passively in the face of unfortunate events and wait for someone else to act, or otherwise refuse to take some personal responsibility where it is feasible.

In short, one man's cardiovascular woes are a tragic genetic inheritance and another's are a result of learned poor choices and acquired external locus of control; one woman's frail skeleton is due to poor diet and another's to her grandmother's poor diet during the Great War. The meaning we ascribe to our experiences, how we respond to internal phenomena, and the relative influence of external factors, are a variable stew. The only common theme may be that these, and many other factors, "run in the family."

Other characteristics, or clusters of behavior, are often attributed to family heritage. Consider the case of Heather, a fourteen-year-old high school student:

> *Heather is failing algebra. She has taken to skipping class, forgetting her homework, and avoiding the free tutoring available after school. "Why should I bother?" she asks*

It Runs in the Family

her guidance counselor. "I stink at math. My whole family does. I can't help it." Does Heather's whole family "stink" at math? How would they know? Both parents dropped out of high school, instead earning their GEDs. Since then, they have both worked hard, and provide well for their family, but neither has a job that requires algebra. They have higher hopes for their children, but Heather seems to think that because she struggles with algebra, and her parents can't help her, that being bad at math just runs in the family, and there is nothing to be done about it. The guidance counselor knows a little about the family. She knows that Heather's father is a successful subcontractor in carpentry, a field that requires excellent applied math skills and a business that requires the ability to keep his accounts in balance. That's hardly the description of someone who just naturally "stinks" at math. Likewise, Heather's mother has built a very solid following as a hairstylist at a salon close to home; creative, competent and professional, she has a waiting list for appointments. Algebra is not part of her job. The challenge for Heather is letting go of her stereotyped thinking. If prodded, what plays in Heather's mind is something like this: my parents can't help me with my homework, therefore they aren't smart enough to do this kind of math. That makes three of us. I can't be good at this stuff; look at my parents. It runs in the family. Heather is assuming lack of a skill (algebra) is something you inherit. Yet, Heather has not inherited the skills her parents have; she cannot build custom cabinets, or create elegant up do's for a bride and her entire wedding party, or manage the accounts and paperwork for a business. Heather is hiding behind her parents and blaming them for her lack of success.

Heather and her guidance counselor need to talk about Heather's underlying belief system and whether it's helping, or hurting, her. Heather has no evidence that her parents are "too dumb" for algebra; she only knows they did not retain it, all these years later. Heather is hurting herself by embracing the myth of math weakness "running in the family."

Toxic Mythology

ANTIDOTES TO THE MYTH

While many things do run in our families, we can free ourselves from the depressing burden of learned helplessness, and equip our children to develop the necessary attitudes and skills to be resilient in the face of difficulties.

Separate physical inheritance from learned habits.

It can be incredibly difficult to sort through what "runs in the family" from enduring poor habits, or even enduring good habits. After all, a slothful person could be postponing developing healthy eating and exercise habits because he doesn't need to:

> Josh, busy with a demanding career and a growing, happy young family doesn't have time to eat right and exercise. His weight has been creeping up, and he finally had to give in and get some new clothes for work. At 40, his blood pressure is elevated, and he's a little more easily fatigued. His wife has been encouraging him to take better care of himself. Josh shrugs off her concerns: look how healthy Pop is, and he's over 65. However, Pop has made a habit of maintaining a weight below his freshman-in-college high point, jogs three times a week, and is active with chores a few hours most days. Pop's robust good health in retirement is not a complete accident. Josh is comforting himself that he has inherited something that is not genetically heritable: his father's entrenched good habits.

In the era of genetic testing, it would be easy enough for Josh to check what his actual predispositions might be. Even without taking that step, he could begin to separate the effects of Pop's disciplined lifestyle from what Josh wishes would be the case for himself. Clearly, if it "ran in the family," Josh, at 40, would be more energetic, trimmer and able to surpass his retired father during the family's backyard football games.

Another piece of this is realizing that even physical inheritances often are affected by lifestyle habits, and learning about how the choices we make impact the expression of physical traits

It Runs in the Family

and tendencies is a source of power. For Josh, beginning a lifestyle of healthier eating and more exercise will yield more energy, improved sleep, sharper concentration, and reduced negative stress symptoms. Because he can relate the improvement to his own choices, he can also enjoy more confidence in his ability to cope with the varying demands of life.

Seek expert guidance on separating the psychological effects of others' bad habits from true inheritances.

When a family exhibits a pattern of addictions, violence and criminality, the child who wants to break free can feel helpless. Look at the family tree: it's a thorny tangle of dysfunction and doom. However, even if there is a genetic predisposition to develop addictions, there is no life sentence. Addictions arise from actions, and action requires a choice.

> *Beth's mother is an alcoholic. Beth's father was addicted to prescription pills, starting with benzodiazepines and ending with morphine. He died of an overdose when Beth was 17. There are other alcoholics and addicts in the extended family. Isolated and ashamed of her home life, Beth spent her adolescence learning the art of being invisible when around the house, tiptoeing past an unconscious parent on the couch when she returned from school, forging parents' signatures on permission slips because they were gone for days, getting high with their "friends." At 25, Beth is having difficulty making lasting friendships. She dreams of being married and having children, but is terrified that she might do what "everyone" says you do when you have alcoholic, addicted parents: you either marry an addict or become one; that's the story. Terrified of inflicting what she suffered on children yet unborn, Beth is paralyzed.*

Beth could benefit from a few important lessons, which will take time to integrate. She may get the light-bulb moment of realization quickly, but undoing the years of believing the myth of hopelessness in the face of such deep family dysfunction will take time and practice. Beth must separate her parents' and other relatives' choices from her own. Help may come from a variety of sources: wise mentors, Al Anon, and a good therapist. Beth will overcome the difficult start by learning to focus on her own strengths and goals, rather than being mired in the past, and by honing her internal sensor for character. Beth will be able to live her own life, discerning good people from dangerous people whose vague similarities to her parents might hold a shimmering attraction and familiarity.

Coach children, and yourself, in the use of the words like "choice," "decision," or "option."

Take every opportunity to refer to the range of options available and emphasizing what you are deciding to do. Avoid saying you "have to" do something unless it really is absolutely necessary. Emphasizing free will may seldom relate to traits that may, or may not, run in the family, but thinking and speaking in this way creates a sense of personal responsibility and power for you, and helps young people develop mental scaffolding to organize their perceptions and decisions in a way that includes personal responsibility rather than mere victimhood.

> *Joey's family tree seems like a labyrinth of health problems. High blood pressure and elevated cholesterol; ulcers, arthritis, and a heavy dose of autoimmune disorders. Certain of these are definitely heritable; others are inherited but are less likely to fully express themselves without Joey's overt cooperation. In other words, by eating a relatively healthy diet, maintaining regular exercise and sleep habits, and using good stress management techniques, Joey can mitigate the inherited tendencies, preventing or at least delaying the onset of diseases that run in the family. In some cases, it may be that lifestyle is the sole cause, in which case Joey will be able to avoid those problems. In other cases, a high-stress, unhealthy lifestyle will provoke high blood pressure, auto-immune disorders, high cholesterol, and type-II diabetes.*

It Runs in the Family

Joey may never develop the conditions that supposedly "run in the family," or one or two may finally make a debut in old age. Unlike siblings who will be limited by the early onset of serious health problems, Joey's deliberate choices will free him for a long, healthy middle age and early old age.

Likewise, the person who asserts that addictions "run in the family" could gain tremendous peace of mind by understanding that developing addictions requires deliberate choices. A person has to decide that the best way to relax at the end of a stressful day is via alcohol, or that coping with social anxiety requires cannabis. These are not spontaneously occurring habits. The tendency to rely on such means to cope with stress is learned, and a person who learns these can choose other, healthier means to cope with stress, anxiety, sadness, or boredom.

What about other, less tangible traits that supposedly run in the family? Heather, our algebra-challenged student, could have benefited from a lifelong lesson in how choices impact outcomes. Heather assumes that not having mastered algebra was caused by her parents not being smart enough to do algebra. She also doesn't understand that her success in algebra rests on several variables. One is the depth of understanding she has chosen to develop about preliminary principles in mathematics. Another is her ability to think abstractly, which is a matter of brain development and is not within our control. Other variables include the quality of instruction and just how hard Heather is willing to work at integrating the new information. Heather's level of brain development, much of which is age-related, is not within her choice. Not all adults are able to work in the theoretical/abstract level of thinking, but we have no evidence yet, at 14, that Heather won't reach this level. Working hard, reviewing preliminary math facts, and seeking tutoring, are all within Heather's control and have no relationship to anything that "runs in the family."

Heather's parents can frame their own choices as choices, rather than as inevitable outcomes. Very often, parents are well aware of the range of choices they're making each day, but fail to communicate this to their children. As a result, children are making choices and unconsciously minimizing the fact that they are choosing. Ask Heather if she is choosing to fail algebra, and she would be indignant. Yet, if she were honest, she is choosing to skip classes; she is choosing to leave her book at school; she is choosing to find other things more compelling than going to the free tutoring after school. In other words, Heather is not overtly choosing to fail algebra, but she is making every minor choice she can to support that outcome.

Heather's parents, meanwhile, are making different choices: to balance the books for their businesses when they might rather watch television or go for a walk; double-checking measurements before cutting either lumber or hair; reading up on the latest trends in their respective fields. Heather isn't paying attention to the choices her parents are making surrounding their success. She is focused on what applies to her, which is their inability to do Algebra. Heather is advertently proving that, her parents' best efforts aside, self-discipline and hard work do not necessarily "run in the family."

2

Free to Be . . . Whatever, Whenever
The Myth of Endless Options

ONE OF THE MYTHS that contributes most directly to personal tragedy is the myth of endless options. Children are told, and far too many adults cling to the belief, that you can be whatever you want to be, or do whatever you want to do, if only you want it badly enough. You can have it all! We need never confine our life with others' imposed limitations; a flowing eternity of opportunities await only the flexion of will.

It is easy to mock the myth with the most basic of examples: I would like very much to have been a professional athlete, perhaps a football player. They earn a lot of money and usually go on to another lucrative career. However, I am female and the approximate size of a jockey. I also have a heart murmur and asthma, so the whole professional athlete option is, and has ever been, out of the question. I want it, though, very badly. Shouldn't that be enough?

The American myth of having it all, and dreams being enough, has evolved over time. Before the mid-1970s, the myth was: you can be whatever you want to be, if you have the ability, the will and the circumstances. This is America; no one can stop you

Toxic Mythology

from fulfilling whatever is your potential. There are a lot of caveats in that myth. The trifecta of aptitude, desire, and external factors must converge. Of course, it was in reality just a feel-good slogan because many people found external factors piled up against them. Would your number came up in the Viet Nam era draft? Did you really have equal access to education and jobs? What were the realities of your family's economics? These are but a few typical contingencies for the myth.

The external factors could be very subtle. Our 8th grade Algebra teacher undermined his female students by only letting the boys know when the before-school enrichment and review sessions were held. It was May before a boy slipped up and mentioned the study sessions in front of the girls. While this teacher did not overtly prevent me, or any other girl, from pursuing any particular career, he did not help matters. Those were the mid-1970s. Young women were getting very mixed messages.

About one year later the smiley faced self-esteem movement reached our little rural burg. Suddenly we were Free to Be You and Me, and We Knew We Were Special, 'Cause God Doesn't Make No Junk. Banks handed out I'm Thumbody stickers instead of lollipops. The myth had evolved from recognizing the limitations of aptitude, desire and external factors. Now everyone was free to be anything. Professional and Olympic athletes gave inspirational speeches to susceptible young people asserting that if we only wanted it badly enough, we, too, could achieve anything we could dream. If you can imagine it, you can do it! If you can dream it, you can have it! What bosh.

We have already alluded to one of the dangerous flaws in this myth: there are cases where the lack of facial validity is comical, as when a smallish woman stamps her foot and whines about wanting to play pro football. In reality, children briefly imagine they can do anything. This is supposed to be a short, magical, and well-supervised period of overblown self-confidence that enables toddlers to let go of Mama's hands. Afterwards, every sensible child is all too aware that she cannot do whatever she wills. The three year old would like very much to scale the kitchen cabinets like

Free to Be . . . Whatever, Whenever

Mount Everest, and breach the cookie jar, but, alas, the little step stool has been locked away since Mama found her toddler nearly achieving this goal. Remember that small children are concrete in their thinking. They are literalists. You tell them that Canada is "over" the United States and they look at the sky; you say the world is round and they worry about rolling off of it. You say, "You can do whatever you want if you want it badly enough," and you are Peter Pan telling them they can fly. By age 7 or 8, however, the child knows you also need, at the least, some pixie dust. Eventually, the child who hears an adult proclaiming the power of desire to reach all imagined goals, absorbs the sense of being a failure. Alternately, the child realizes the adult is either stupid, crazy or lying.

The issue of stupid, crazy or lying grownups is an important one in children's psychological development. Children need to feel that their adults are sensible and trustworthy. Adults who are foolish, psychotic or dishonest are scary to children, because an unhinged adult renders the world unpredictable and unsafe. It is vital that children feel the world is a safe place. Safety and security are imperative for maximized development of skills, intellect and emotional strength. When a child's emotional energy is invested in seeking security, it is less available to learn and explore.

Another sort of damage results from the long, painful time it can take to be willing, and able, to face the fact that it was the adult spouting the myth who was flawed, and not the child who failed to achieve a goal.

> *Tony is abused by the other kids at school, surreptitiously, every day. A push here, a shove there, some ostracism, and even a little forcible eating of dirt. Dad says Tony should be able to stand up to those boys, and learn to get along with them. Alas, all the pep talks in the world will not change the bullying in Tony's life. Research tells us that if Tony could develop one friendship he would be much safer at school, but Tony knows very well that, having been selected to be the whipping boy of bullies, his worth as a potential friend has plummeted and even another outcast will be reluctant to attract the attention of bullies by befriending Tony. All the confidence and newfound social acumen in the world,*

Toxic Mythology

> on Tony's part, cannot make other children behave differently. He has influence but no control over them, and influence only to the degree that he is willing, and able, to do something effective. He may also begin to suspect that many adults are stupid, or indifferent, or both, as no one seems to notice how deeply he suffers. Tony is learning that kids are mean and that his parents must be very disappointed in him, indeed, since he is such a loser and cannot follow their advice to make other people like him.

This is another danger of the myth: the creation of shame where none need exist. Children naturally experience shame when they don't meet adult expectations; a little healthy shame about dirty diapers is what finally leads to successful potty training. The embarrassment of having to give back the small shoplifted item and apologize at age 5 or 6 burns that experience into memory, along with its corollary: don't steal and this won't happen again. Children don't need to feel shame over normal parts of themselves, but the myth of being whatever you want, if only you want it badly enough, is a recipe for shame long after childhood.

The myth has some positive roots and essential truths: there is no doubt that potential for each individual person often far exceeds the grasp taken. When you consider the depth of education achieved by George Washington at age 16, it's easy to see that the average US sophomore is not pulling her weight, in terms of reaching her potential, despite having vastly more resources and study time. Even so, every person does not have the aptitude for every possible occupation, art, athletic skill, or type of personality.

The myth, of course, does not take into account another very real factor: the absolute limitations of time and space. It is a truth nearly universally denied, that one cannot have everything one wants, and certainly not in the order in which desired. For the past forty years or so, this truth has been treated as a sort of heresy. Instead, young people have been lulled into believing that not only can they have the outcomes they seek, they can have them at a timing of their choosing. Each new generation seems to believe this, despite the appalling fall-out among their parents, or those old enough to be their parents. We cannot have it all, and we cannot have even what little we may get in whatever order we prefer.

When the wall of reality is hit at midlife, there are biological and psychological facts at play that mean that earlier choices were not just passing fancies and errors. There is not a perpetual reset button on life; you cannot endlessly reboot this system. Those early choices bear permanent effects, and those effects corral the options available. It is not an exaggeration to call the adjustment to reality a grieving process.

Middle-aged adults who pursued their parents' goals for them sometimes realize that the career they have has never, and will never, fit their disposition or talents. They would like to change tracks, but some changes are not possible. The training for some professions, such as the medical fields, requires not only tremendous time and willpower, but the capacity to memorize vast quantities of data. This is called fluid intelligence. It tends to peak early, slowly declining starting by age 40, although the first bits of this reduced ability to remember facts and figures, quickly, is often camouflaged by the increase in crystal and analytic intelligence. Crystal intelligence (knowledge) and analytic ability increase and remain at a plateau into the sixties or later, and may continue very effectively until senescence. This is a good reason to send the latest White House spokesperson to the store with a verbal list of groceries, or want him on your team for Trivial Pursuit or Jeopardy, but you had better ask Dr. Kissinger to explain the implications of recent events involving the Muslim Brotherhood and Coptic Christians on Israeli-Palestinian negotiations. The brilliant woman who sailed through nursing school, and became an ARNP in her late twenties, can find that pursuing her real dream — to be a physician — is an entirely different matter twenty-odd years later. It may not be impossible, but the challenge of memorization and long hospital shifts are substantial for anyone: more for someone in midlife than in young adulthood. Willpower cannot trump physiology.

The tragedy of infertility is perhaps the most heart-rending outcome of believing or fooling oneself with, the lie that there is always plenty of time, and we can really have it all. The biological truth is that female fertility plummets in the late twenties. Neither is male fertility an endless field of opportunity. Fold in the effects of often silent sexually transmitted diseases, and the result is the profound sorrow of couples, where each partner decided to "enjoy their youth and freedom" and to be "successful" before beginning a family. They must now accept that having children is one option that may have been effectively removed from the table.

As tragic as the grief over opportunities surrendered is the awareness that there was sometimes not a tradeoff that even begins to merit the sacrifice. To have dedicated oneself to a cause—military or missionary, for example—and have the awareness of that higher purpose as the counterbalance to losses later, can provide the basis for psychological and spiritual adjustment. Realizing you have given up the career of your dreams and your hopes of a family to have "fun," whatever that may mean, is a very hollow source of satisfaction in middle age, when the evenings are long and quiet, and the years are short. Spending the first twenty years of adulthood getting drunk, high and trying to get "lucky" often bears three rotten fruits: an arrested character development that makes the individual in question highly undesirable as a mate; some sort of souvenir infection with various unpleasant effects; and a dearth of stories of any interest to anyone who is neither drunk nor stoned.

Pursuing professional success, or the wrong career, or money, as if acquiring a large pile of wealth were required before beginning marriage and a family, are generally unnecessary. There are very few career options in which absolute youth is necessary, and these are short-lived: professional athletes and fashion models, for example, although both athletes and models marry and have children. Sometimes people pursue one career and then another. The idea that hopping from field to field is easy, something we can achieve if we merely want it badly enough, is hazardous to happiness. While there are certainly people capable of pursuing advanced degrees in multiple fields, and some succeed in doing so, the fact is, many professions require such length and depth of study, and such exhausting expense, that only a highly gifted

Free to Be... Whatever, Whenever

person with unusual circumstances is apt to have that combination of aptitude, desire and external factors. Most people cannot pay off the student loans of medical school and dive into a doctoral program in family therapy, or law, or microbiology. There is simply not enough time to go around, nor is there sufficient money to pay for the process.

We used to all know this: that making a choice meant you were abandoning many other choices. Marrying one person meant, supposedly, forsaking all others. Having children meant focusing on the children with less energy available, for the time being, to develop a career. Electing to major in chemical engineering meant you were not going to pursue a career in art restoration. You might love art restoration, but most engineering programs are too competitive to allow you to wander off to remote locales to do internships in the careful restoration of old art, or volunteer at the local museum to the exclusion of engineering projects. It is a buffet of options, but you don't have unlimited refills. Whether large choices or small, each choice leads inescapably to a shift in subsequent options.

This self-evident truth is not so clear to children. They only gradually develop the capacity for abstract, that is, not-literal thought, if at all. If a child is burdened with the ego-stroking of grade inflation, and that narcissistic fire is stoked with the myth that he can be whatever he wants if he only wants it badly enough, the stage is set for some very dire disappointments and raw, narcissistic rage when reality breaks through the bubble.

> *Suzanne gets "As" on all her science projects. The science projects are indeed wonderful, as they should be: mom, who has a BS in microbiology, "helps." Suzanne sails through elementary and middle school with As. She is planning on passing all the AP science exams she can. Because AP courses have been a bit watered down via an injection of social commentary, Suzanne may be able to pass with less absolute knowledge of biology than her mother needed 25 years ago. Mom, of course, doesn't know that: she's bought the notion that kids now have to work much harder at school than any previous generation, although very few*

> are finishing their education and working as surveyors and mapmakers in the wilderness, with primitive equipment, as George Washington was—at age 16.
>
> Suzanne goes off to college, still believing she is capable of anything, and can do or be whatever she wants, if she only wants it badly enough. She is surrounded by young people who have been taught the same thing, but some of them have already had to put sweat into their success. Her competitors' experience in working, and willingness to exert considerable effort, is an external factor in Suzanne's life that may not be an issue until late in her bachelor's program or graduate studies. Suzanne did not expect to compete with students who were experienced in making the kinds of day-to-day decisions in which one thing they wanted very much (enough sleep, a date, or pizza with friends) was subjugated to something else they wanted (an A on a microbiology exam).

I have had students at every level, from elementary through doctoral programs, assert they want an "A" but then express unwillingness and resentment at the effort expected. Why should they have to work so hard? They *want* an A. They *tried*. Don't they get points for effort?

The fact is that what passes for "effort" is often not much effort at all. In a class of 40, I may see 5 or 10 taking notes. Some have no paper, no pencil, and no textbook in evidence. They believe that by showing up they are making a serious effort. It is not politically correct to say so, but work, temperament and aptitude are critical. These factors are not in the myth, after all; the myth is all about wishing and daydreaming. Daydreaming about one's eventual success is not useful during class.

Some fields require intense, focused study. An extreme extrovert, who requires lots of interaction with other people, will find hours of quiet study torturous. That's not to say that a gregarious person cannot make it through post-doctoral work in a subfield of physics, but it will be harder to climb into the deep analytical work required. Conversely, an introvert will find certain fields challenging on the basis of temperament, even when aptitude and interest are present. Aptitude is not just intelligence as an IQ score, but also the type of intelligence: some people can memorize a great deal while others are far more analytical. A slightly-above-average IQ of 115 combined with an excellent memory lends itself to medical school but is not sufficient for quantum physics.

Since our choices inherently close other doors of opportunity, the issue of "fit" in selecting goals is a critical success factor. All too often, "fit" is reduced to what seems attractive due to superficial aspects of the career: earning potential or the respect afforded those in the profession. Most likely, relying on aptitude tests to determine what the child will be good at doing is given weight. This is not a sufficient measure, as aptitude may cross many fields that are very poor fits for the child's temperament and personality.

Occasionally, this discussion occurs regarding the needs of gifted children. Academically gifted children often "flat line," that is, score with high aptitude across multiple fields in career testing. It does no good to tell a highly gifted child that since she seems equally capable of doing the work of neuroscience, civil engineering and archeology, she ought to pick the one that pays the best. A child can excel in an area on a standardized test and still find it painfully uninteresting. The lecture that she should want to use her gifts to the best of her ability is a potentially dangerous corollary to the "be whatever you want to be" myth. This subset asserts that other people definitely know what is the "best use" and dismisses the desire part of the myth. The child is reduced to raw material for the collective, like a Soviet child tracked into a career with no options. Here, though, the child is given a dose of guilt if she doesn't want to live up to her ability. An interesting example can be found in the occasional article positing that college educations are "wasted" on stay-at-home mothers: apparently, it is a priori that the education, and the woman, are squandered on something the authors of those articles deem inconsequential: nurturing the next generation.

So, we have our myth: you can be whatever you want to be, if you only want it enough, and if your advisors decide it is the best use of your talents. Shame on you for not wanting something badly enough; if you really wanted it, you would have made it happen, wouldn't have you? Thus, failure to achieve is a lack of willpower — unless something sinister is at play.

Cognitive dissonance arises from clinging to two separate and incompatible facts. It take a lot of effort at distraction, every day, for an intelligent person to ignore cognitive dissonance. There are, based on my experience over years of work as a therapist and instructor, an alarming number of people who can concurrently believe the primary myth that you can be whatever you will, if you only want it enough, and the myth that failure to achieve a fantasized goal must inherently be due to malevolence. They on one hand buy into the myth that desire alone should yield positive outcomes and simultaneously, thanks to a complete unwillingness to live an examined life, buy into the convenient external locus of control, in which one gets to be the innocent flotsam tossed about by forces that are inexplicably and selectively malignant or benign. If you think you wished hard enough, and did not achieve it anyway, then the problem lies outside you and someone else must have blocked you. It was that teacher, that employer, that coach who held you back and thwarted your will for success. Failure to achieve a desired goal must be due to deliberate malevolence. This corollary part of the myth feeds resentment and bitterness. There may be malevolence; if so, certainly wishing will not make this cease. Merely wishing will certainly not adequately address the need for hard work, resourcefulness, persistence, and other patterns of actions needed to succeed in the face of normal challenges, much less malevolence. When the mental set of wish v. malevolence = someone else's fault I did not succeed, cognitive dissonance is at play.

The tolerance for cognitive dissonance past the age of reason is a source of many problems. In the case of this particular myth and its corollaries, many people display an impressive ability to ignore the psychic discomfort caused by maintaining a desperate grip on conflicting philosophical positions. Cognitive dissonance should be painful; the pain is supposed to lead to reflective thought and a clarification of position. Our society tends to support coping

Free to Be... Whatever, Whenever

with cognitive dissonance the way it encourages managing every other kind of discomfort: via distraction and numbing. Drugs, alcohol and an incessant flood of electronic media are very effective at diverting people from the natural discomfort of cognitive dissonance. This includes the contrast between reality and political correctness.

It is not politically correct to say that sometimes, for reasons we cannot understand, things are not fair. One person is born in the United States and another in a refugee camp in South Sudan. One person is both good-looking and brilliant, and another is plain and dull. Life is not fair, and neither are people. Because the truth does sting, and, for reflective people, raises existential dilemmas, it is more comfortable to turn to the false myths.

A myth carries the seed of truths. We do have within us much more capacity than any of us realize. Aptitude alone is not sufficient: a brilliant child working on the family fishing boat in South Viet Nam, whose reflective and analytic abilities far exceed most people's capacities, will never have the opportunity to shine on a series of high school exams and win a scholarship to the best science school in the world. The external factors are not present, despite the aptitude and the desire to live the life of the mind. Desire is an important factor. It is necessary but not sufficient, and it is the inadequacy in our popular mythology of that second part of the fact—the insufficiency of desire—that makes a critical difference.

The same malicious disregard for reality and human nature that has been drumming the have-it-all message into our children has taken the dream of a healthy, happy adulthood and turned it into some sort of Gotterdammerung. What does it mean when marriage and a family is viewed as something best left to when you are just too old and tired to have fun, as if a mate and children were some sort of chore on par with cleaning toilets and figuring out the precise source of the puddle under the kitchen sink? The message often seems to be, if you're going to try to have it all, then once you're too old to get out there and get lucky, you may have to settle for a quiet night at home, tucking in the babies and resting in the arms of someone who would die for you.

Toxic Mythology

THE ANTIDOTES:

Change your language to change your thinking.

As with many of the toxic myths, the first step is to challenge and change vocabulary. It is not cruelly limiting to say to a child, or yourself, "You could choose from so many wonderful careers!" instead of, "You can be anything you want, if you want it badly enough!" Framing choices in terms of what is possible and desirable is, in fact, empowering.

> Suzanne finishes up her first semester at college with C's, a withdrawal, and one incomplete, granted by a well-intended instructor who hopes that the lessons of having earned poor grades and squandered much of the first semester at college will be useful and that Suzanne will use the extra 30 days to complete course work well. Resentful, and angry at her professors, Suzanne buries her nascent shame at her own performance beneath complaints about unclear instructions, unfair grading, and too much work. Suzanne's mother, her erstwhile assistant, has a few choices here. She can remain a neutral listener; she can commiserate with her self-pitying formerly-A student, or she can change the words. Imagine the challenge to Suzanne's unreasonable expectations if Mom's responses fall along the lines of:
>
> "Yes, it's hard to focus on academics when there seem to be so many fun activities. It must have been tempting to keep putting off studying." (There's no reason to rub it in; Suzanne is well aware that, at this juncture, it is clear this was a suboptimal choice.)
>
> "It is unfortunate that you decided to dedicate so little time to your studies."
>
> "How do you plan to budget your time next semester?"
>
> "What will you have to do differently to earn the kind of grades you want?"
>
> "What did you do differently in your 'C' course than in your 'Withdrawn' course that you could use to be successful in more classes next term?"

Free to Be . . . Whatever, Whenever

With the emphasis on Suzanne's choices, rather than on what "happened to her," Suzanne might shift from imagining herself a victim of capricious college instructors to being in charge of her academic journey. The grades were not "given" to her, nor were her wasted evenings and weekends things that just "happened." Every moment, she made choices in which she set herself up for failure, rather than success. If she chose failure, she could instead choose success.

Building on the change in language, remember that other people's outcomes represent numerous small choices.

Breaking down the choices is critical to understanding that often people don't really want what they say they want. Guide children and adolescents in learning to break down the big pictures to see the connections between goals, small steps, and outcomes.

While external circumstances certainly affect outcomes, there are numerous other choices, often deceptively small, that accrue to large decisions, accumulating to influence the results we experience in life. All sorts of resources, including the allocation of time, are in play. Each moment, you make a choice. On a Saturday morning, the only opportunity you have to use that particular slice of the space/time continuum, you make a tremendous range of choices. Get up for an early morning jog? Go to work and give it your best? Sleep off a hangover? Be up before the kids so you can make pancakes together and then have fun playing at gardening? Each choice precipitates other choices. Make a choice often enough, and it becomes a habit, and some of those habits will preclude certain outcomes. Research supports what professionals have long suggested: regular use of cannabis leads to a lack of initiative that does not remit when marijuana use stops. In other words, the regular pot-smoker may be choosing to become a lifelong slacker, even when "clean." The regular, or even occasional, pot-smoker may be choosing to become permanently anxious or even psychotic, if there is a slight predisposition and vulnerability. These are choices, among many, that are not retractable. Make the choice often enough, and it can be impossible to choose an alternative.

> Matthew wants to be an astronaut. He is 12. He loves science fiction, and he excels at science in school. He is hoping to go to Space Camp over the summer. Matthew imagines he is putting everything into place to be an astronaut. Matthew's parents are encouraging his dreams and praising him for having a high goal. They are also failing to help Matthew understand that certain choices he's making now will almost guarantee he will never be an astronaut. Matthew would rather play space-themed video games than run, jump, climb, and play outdoors. Matthew is also experimenting with marijuana and occasionally borrows a friend's ADHD medication to help him study. The effects of substance abuse and a sedentary lifestyle will interfere with Matthew's physical and mental fitness. He is actively undermining the dream that he's been told, repeatedly, is achievable, if only he wants it badly enough. Does he want to be an astronaut badly enough to begin pursuing physical fitness, eschewing drugs, and tearing himself away from the video games?

Would it hurt Matthew to hear, repeatedly, from multiple sources, that achieving his dream will require not just wishing and some good luck, but also day-to-day changes in his actions, even now, at age 12? Matthew is being unfairly buffered from the harsh reality that each day, he is making countless small choices that build a barrier between him and his astronaut dreams.

Children are not the only ones who need these messages. As adults, it can be easy to overlook the choices and sacrifices involved in anyone else's life. We see the successful business owner and the trappings: the nice car, the nice house, the "freedom" we imagine comes with "being your own boss." Of course, to the business owner, there is no such thing as a paid vacation, or employer-paid benefits, or time when she is really "off." She is not her own boss; every customer is her boss, and every unhappy customer a distressingly displeased boss. When the onlooker imagines how great it would be to be in her shoes, all those other variables need

Free to Be . . . Whatever, Whenever

to be weighed, too. Do you really want the nice car enough to give up weekends of peace and escape from work? Will the nice house compensate for the 70 hour work week? What about the years of sacrificing a personal life to build that business; do you want to make that trade, too?

Do the homework to develop realistic, and idealistic, dreams for yourself. Guide young people to use the same techniques in developing goals that are achievable, noble, and fit well.

Matthew, our 12-year-old aspiring astronaut, may not actually know what being an astronaut entails. He no doubt imagines all sorts of glamorous, exciting work of piloting space ships and doing space walks. The routine of maintenance, recuperating from the bone-and-muscle depleting effects of zero gravity, and other aspects of the work no doubt evade him entirely or are minimized. He may not realize that some of his developing personality traits are incompatible with being an astronaut, or at least would be a constant challenge for him.

We seldom think about goodness of fit when we consider life choices. Yet, a lifestyle that embraces a person's abilities, values and personality is most likely to lead to life filled with meaning, purpose and happiness. Making choices based not just on emotions, and possible aptitudes, but also on personality and values, would be a vast improvement.

> Don, a gifted high school senior with an IQ over 140, has near-perfect SAT scores and a 3.95 GPA. Based on the aptitude testing, he has "flat-lined," or topped out in numerous areas. According to the tests, Don would be just as competent as a chemical engineer as a neurosurgeon. Don's parents and guidance counselor are pressuring him to maximize his potential income and status by applying to the best programs in pre-med and engineering. If Don acquiesces, he may very well find himself depressed, anxious, and floundering. This is because Don's personality is poorly suited for these particular professions. He would be

Toxic Mythology

> an excellent fit as a psychotherapist or clergy. If his parents are status-oriented, they may discourage him from careers that will result in lower opportunities for material success. Psychology and religious vocations are unlikely to yield worldly success, but they are a good fit for Don.

Using a variety of assessments that measure interests and affinities, rather than aptitude, opens the door to a better understanding of choices that will fit. Rather than trying to force ourselves to be the square peg in a round hole, we can develop a vision for the square hole that fits us well and encourages, rather than tries to squeeze out, the elements of us that are unique and important.

The Self-Directed Search™ is a commonly used career questionnaire that focuses much more on goodness of fit than on skills. It generates lists of general interest areas and, by combining sets of them, lists careers according to how members of those careers matched up with the general categories of interests and abilities. Don, for example, would have shown a high level of Social interest, meaning concern for and willingness to work with others. It also lists the careers by how much education is required, so Don knows that people with response patterns similar to his might become psychotherapists or clergy, or they may become daycare workers, depending on their willingness and ability to pursue post-secondary training. This doesn't mean that Don can't become a chemical engineer; he may pursue this and be aware that he has to feed some aspects of his personality through other endeavors. The difference, in this case, is that the chemical engineering field may not address Don's creative drive and social interest sufficiently. If Don accommodates to this via deliberate choices, he will begin to create a life that is full and fits him. His fulltime career might meet his need for intellectually challenging work, and, via volunteering and avocations, he could enrich his life and find great meaning and purpose. Alternately, he could allow himself to be forced into a career that is not a good fit, be bitter and resentful, and feel unable to make a midlife change because too much has been invested, literally and figuratively, in his education and career.

Free to Be ... Whatever, Whenever

Video games, substance abuse and mediocrity ought not be the apex of youthful daydreams, but imagining that energy invested in these will result in a life of wealth, power and personal fulfillment is not the alternative. The truth, that we have the potential to be and do so much more than seems possible, merits dedicated retelling.

3

You Should Go Out, and Not Be So Antisocial

PEOPLE INTERRUPT CONVERSATIONS WITH one person to respond to a text message from another. They use profane language, dress inappropriately for the circumstances (gym clothes at the office, pajamas at the 8 AM lecture class), become publicly inebriated, and bully one another. General tolerance for these and other misbehaviors, even double-dipping tortilla chips, seems high. Some social sins, though, are inexcusable.

The worst offenses, in the social milieu, comprise any behaviors that seem antisocial. The word is tossed around very freely. The shy student, the introvert, the quiet neighbor who dares to mind his own business and go quietly about his day with just a wave, a smile and a hello, are all deemed *antisocial*.

There are so many errors in this thinking, so many false myths converging dangerously, that it really takes several books, such as Susan Cain's *Quiet* and Martha Stout's *The Sociopath Next Door*, to adequately break down the many misconceptions and erroneous definitions. This chapter will attempt to summarize the problem, challenge the myth, and offer solutions.

You Should Go Out, and Not Be So Antisocial

Imagine that you have two neighbors. Bill lives on your right, and Kate on your left. Kate is friendly and charming. She waves hello, stops to chat, admires your azaleas ("How do you get them to bloom for so long?") and has invited your household over to join hers for some lemonade on the deck. She is witty and observant, complimenting your shaggy calico cat, who has a bad habit of slipping out your backdoor and disappearing for hours at a time.

Bill is quiet. He comes and goes, will give a quick wave and perhaps say hello. His yard is neat, his house is quiet. He isn't exactly a hermit, per se; you do see friends coming and going, and they all seem quite happy to see one another. You overhear lively snippets of conversations on every topic under the sun, wafting across the back fence. Still, Bill doesn't seem to quite 'fit in' in the neighborhood. No one really knows much about him. He is, everyone concurs, despite the evidence of his frequent visitors, kind of a loner.

When you are inexplicably delayed at work on trash day, and find your empty cans were dragged up the driveway and the lids placed carefully on them, you surmise a neighbor took care of it and assume it was Kate. If you thank her, she will probably say, "No problem," without a blink. When Maxwell the Cat dies and the vet suggests the cat ingested poisoned food, you drive home numbly, get out of your car, stare around your illusorily benign neighborhood and suspect . . . Bill. He is, after all, the loner. Yet there is nothing in anything Bill has done to indicate he hates cats, or is cruel and sadistic. He has been nothing less than a good neighbor (including dragging up your trash cans and putting your neglected, sunburned paper on your front porch), but, he is . . . a loner. He's nothing like Kate, who is bubbly and engaging but whom, if you thought about it, you don't actually know very well at all. She's fun to talk with, but as to her actual beliefs, or her past, or much of anything, it seems very vague. Kate, however, probably knows a lot, and perhaps too much, about you.

You don't know Bill. You have never rescued his trash cans on a windy day. If you had ever tended to his mailbox when he was away, you'd have noticed he supports the local animal shelter

Toxic Mythology

(where he also volunteers), making him an unlikely candidate for poisoning Maxwell the Cat. You actually haven't been a very good neighbor to Bill, but he doesn't hold it against you. He, meanwhile, has been a good neighbor, but you don't realize it. Kate has been more than happy to take credit for Bill's quiet thoughtfulness whenever you offer it.

This is because Kate is *antisocial*. Antisocial means something very specific, and very bad. In psychiatric parlance, antisocial means exactly what it would seem to mean if you break the word down to its components: the person is against society. Not indifferent to it, or detached, or only marginally engaged, but deliberately and calculatingly against society. In earlier decades, psychiatry used psychopath and sociopath to label those whom we now call antisocial. The parameters, however, are the same. For the sake of brevity, in this chapter, I will use the acronyms ASP (antisocial person) and INNIE (for introvert). The appropriateness of the term ASP will become clear.

Kate is an ASP. Bill is an INNIE.

The ASP has little to no interest in relationships with others except to the degree to which those relationships meet his needs. ASPs do not experience empathy, or remorse. Actions that appear to be empathic or kind are done as part of the method of building connections and a structure for manipulation. An ASP might have a dog and care for the dog as a means to meet possible sexual partners at the doggie park. The ASP will probably be charming, engaging, and even seductive; ASPs often are. One cannot obtain victims for manipulation, exploitation, or (far less commonly) violence very easily without a good charm offensive. The ASP will carefully assess the object of his attention: what kind of woman is this? What are the ways to manipulate her, draw her in, work her over for money, gifts, attention, etc.? As observant as the best of salespeople and better at reading people than many psychotherapists, the ASP draws a victim in like Kaa in Disney's version of Kipling's "The Jungle Book," luring prey with the somnolence-inducing, "Trust in me . . . "

You Should Go Out, and Not Be So Antisocial

ASPs, in other words, appear outgoing, friendly, engaging, and fun. They are interested in you, which feels wonderful, until you become aware that they are interested in you in the way a coyote is interested in a rabbit.

Often, popular people have a streak of antisocial behavior, if not the whole set of traits. A little inflated self-regard is part of what modern Americans admire as charisma; a quick put-down has become an easy replacement for cleverness. Many people laugh at others' mistakes, gape at auto accident victims, and find torture-porn movies entertaining. Others' misfortunes, real or imagined, are diversions. Cleverly cruel antiheroes are the protagonists of entertainment. Drug dealers, serial killers, and motorcycle gangs are television heroes. Decadence is idealized.

The human attraction towards badness and power starts early. Childhood bullies have this streak of antisocial tendency, and are often seen as popular by their peers. Children become bullies by learning to dominate and manipulate others. They are often seen as leaders, and certainly have followers. The adults around them seldom see the subterranean cruelties that keep the apparently adoring posse under control. The child-bully grows into the adult bully, who may continue to be mildly antisocial or blossom into a full blown case of antisocial personality disorder: cruel, indifferent or perhaps entertained by the suffering of others, manipulative and shrewd. However, the adult ASP often has a charming veneer that keeps people from seeing the viper's nest that substitutes for a human heart. The impulsive behaviors, such as suddenly moving or quitting a job, are constructed into a narrative of justifiable indignation and the only honorable choice. It's the untenable situation, not the irresponsibility of the ASP, which is to blame for the wake of destruction and chaos. While the specific outcomes of studies on psychiatric problems in incarcerated populations varies, there is no doubt that antisocial personality disorder is well-represented in prisons. Recent research indicates over 1/3 of prisoners meet the criteria for Antisocial Personality Disorder; other studies suggest a figure closer to 47%. ASPs are sometimes merely manipulative acquaintances or heart-breaking ex-lovers; others are violent criminals. The mental structures and deficits remain constant: deceit, remorselessness, and an inability to experience empathy.

Introverts (INNIEs), on the other hand, are quite a different sort of person. Introversion is simply one side of a continuum that comprises extreme extroversion and extreme introversion. It is, in most ways, a typical bell curve of distribution but skews towards extroversion in the United States. In some cultures, such as Japan, the skew is towards introversion. Introversion and extroversion are biologically based personality traits and are linked to other traits, neurologically. Genetic research has found that certain biomarkers link sensory sensitivity, creativity, introversion and ectomorphism. Introverts are more sensitive to the environment. Compared to an extrovert, the introvert's experience of a typical social venue is one of being pelted by overwhelming sensory input. The electrical currents in the brain are doing a feverish cha-cha, compared to the languorous, relaxing experience of the extrovert. Introversion and its oft-times partner trait of intuitiveness, tend to correlate highly with above-average intelligence.

Your neighbor, Bill, then, is an INNIE. Apt to be sensitive to the environment and to others, he is quiet. It takes "less" for him to have "enough," whether it's noise, lights, or social activity. Conversations with friends, as you surmise over the back fence, are lengthy, deep and passionate, punctuated with exclamations and laughter. In fact, the degree of active engagement he shows with friends makes him seem all the more suspicious to his neighbors; what makes him seem so rude to the neighbors? Is he a snob?

Yes, the INNIE is often considered a snob. This begins in elementary school, too. If about 2/3 of the children skew towards extroversion, and this is the means to make the necessary social connections for emotional survival at school, introverts and shy children are both at disadvantages. While the introvert gets overwhelmed at preschool and withdraws to a quiet corner with a picture book for a few moments to hit an internal reset button, the extroverts are interacting, albeit not always successfully. Preschoolers are not very skilled at collaborative play yet, but it hardly matters. The introverted child, who will interact with others successfully but also will play peacefully and purposefully alone, seems like the odd tot out to worried parents and teachers.

Bill may be a snob, or he may simply find the loud, busy block parties that end at 1 AM too much. He would like very much to sit and have a good conversation with one or two people at a time, digging into some topic, and sharing ideas. He's not much for the superficial, socially facile environment of large gatherings. In a neighborhood dominated by extroverts, Bill's particular strengths don't show. The myth that those who are less sociable are antisocial has predisposed his neighbors to misinterpret his quiet, reserved friendliness as something sinister. INNIEs are scary to people who have been poisoned with the myth of the antisocial introvert.

There are, of course, antisocial introverts, but the existence of a Unibomber does not mean that every bright and introverted person is plagued with psychopathology. There seems to be little research to support that, and substantially more supporting the extroversion-ASP connection.

Is this myth really such a source of trouble? Indeed, it can be. Let us assume our children grow up immersed in the myth that the quiet person is antisocial. The risks include mistaking superficial traits for character, misjudging both good and bad people, and undervaluing one's own strengths.

In a world that values superficial aspects of a good personality and social graces, it is easy to grant a positive bias towards the extroverted person. Charm is mistaken for good character; enthusiasm for initiative; impulsivity for creativity. It is easy to mistake one for the other without careful observation and reflection, and ours is not a culture given to either of these processes. It's far easier to go by surface clues (which ASPs are expert at generating) than to really think about conversations later, reflecting on our own internal reactions and processes. So the smiling, chatty neighbor who says little that doesn't seem to directly match with your wants or expectations, but whose eyes have something a little odd, a bit unblinking and cool about them, seems nice, while the quiet neighbor is judged deficient.

Toxic Mythology

It may not make much of a difference in neighbors, unless you are debating whom to have check on the house while you're traveling. The inability to discern ASPs from INNIEs, though, will make a profound difference when dating, working, and trying to develop friendships.

Children who are raised to interpret quietness as something negative will be drawn to apparently outgoing people. There is nothing wrong with this, of course; different personality types are attractive to different people. Healthy people don't want to find themselves in relationships with ASPs, but often do. They have been taught to disregard their gut feelings (see the chapter on judging), and to value surface over substance. In a world in which nearly 10% of teenagers experience violence in "romantic" relationships we have a lot of young people who find themselves surprised, apparently, when bitten, figuratively, by an ASP.

> *In October, 2013, 22-year-old Brianna Anderson of Tampa, Florida was shot, "execution style," by her supposed boyfriend, a convicted felon named Jamar Silas. She was briefly revived by emergency personnel and her unborn child delivered by emergency C-section. Ms. Anderson left behind a 3-year-old son and a newborn daughter. It is a tragic story for her, for the children, and for the people who loved them. It is all the more tragic because it is almost certain that this young woman knew that the man she lived with was a dangerous, violent human being. For reasons we cannot know, she decided it was worth tolerating the risk to have his company and chose to pair-bond with an ASP.*

While I cannot know for sure her killer is antisocial, we know he has an established criminal history as a felon. We know that, after at least one conviction for felony, he continued to disregard the law—a warning sign of antisocial personality disorder—by having a firearm despite the prohibition against felons possessing firearms. He murdered her, apparently in the presence of a 3-year-old child, showing profound disregard for the life of Brianna and her children.

Young people need to learn to discern psychopathology, and stop confusing it with introversion. Young women who can tell a sociopath from a good person are less likely to be abused; young men who are not swayed by manipulation are apt to choose healthy relationships.

THE ANTIDOTES

Replace the vocabulary that discriminates against introversion and properly label what you are experiencing and observing. In doing so, learn to identify antisocial behaviors.

When "antisocial" is used as a synonym for reserved, shy, quiet, humble, modest, self-effacing, dignified, private, and, yes, introverted, we are using the label of severe pathology—something shared by nearly 50% of convicted criminals in prisons, by some measures—to describe healthy human functioning.

Imagine Bill, the quiet neighbor, if the other residents didn't confuse "antisocial" with Bill's actual character:

> Bill, who lives on the second house on the block, seems like a nice guy. He's quiet, that's for sure, but he has a lot of friends. He's a good neighbor, too; I've seen him dragging in others' trash cans on windy days. He climbed on the roof the rescue Maxwell the Cat for us after Maxwell somehow got stranded there, evading a stray dog. He loves animals—turns out he volunteers at the local shelter almost every weekend. Who knew? I guess he's just not the sort to go around blowing his own horn. Yes, Bill's a great guy. He's not much for big gatherings—he'll tell you so himself—but one-on-one, he's friendly and he'd do anything for you. And, hey, he doesn't make a lot of noise. Who could ask for more in a neighbor?

Toxic Mythology

What about Kate, the charming, friendly neighbor? Would she look so perfect, if Bill wasn't being denigrated for being the quiet type?

> Yes, Kate's friendly enough. We've been over there several times to visit. What is she like? Well, come to think of it . . . I don't really know. We have a lot of fun, lots of laughs, but . . . I don't really know much about her. How odd.

Yes, it's odd, unless you understand that the objective of a sociopath is not to build a deep understanding, but to grow to understand you enough to manipulate you, exploit you, or just practice those techniques at your expense. Remember the ASP is interested in you in the way the coyote is interested in the rabbit.

There are warning signs for antisocial personality disorder. ASPs are often superficially charming, very relaxed and calm. For all their surface charm and apparent intelligence, they seem to be wandering aimlessly through life, with no lasting attachments or sustained plans. Careful observers will notice a tendency to be unreliable, dishonest, and unconcerned about their actions' effects on others. While charming and glib, there doesn't seem to be any depth to the emotions the ASP expresses. Romantic attachments are for sexual convenience, rather than a pursuit of relationship. There can also be sudden, and seemingly excessive, incidents of rage and violence. Emotional outbursts of anger can seem to come out of the blue. Poisoning Maxwell the Cat because he defecated in her garden seems perfectly reasonable to Kate; shooting his "girlfriend" probably seemed justifiable in the mind of Brianna's murderer. Of course, not all ASPs murder their girlfriends or poison pets. Sometimes they are grown-up versions of school-yard bullies, and they have the power to make life miserable:

> Amber and Jessica are roommates in an off-campus apartment. Acquaintances in high school, they are now hundreds of miles from home. Amber, outgoing, popular and charming, sometimes deigns to bring Jessica, who is a bit anxious and shy, along to parties and bars. Amber will sometimes instruct Jessica to "not be annoying," just

You Should Go Out, and Not Be So Antisocial

before they go into an event; at other times she will abandon Jessica in public or at a house party, leaving without her. She has made it a point to establish contact with Jessica's friends via social media, telling them how "weird" and "psycho" Jessica is. Amber posts rude remarks about Jessica's appearance and personality flaws, knowing Jessica will see them. Isolated and far from home, Jessica tends to blame herself for her troubles, and, when the semester and her tranquility are shattered, only belatedly begins to realize that her roommate is an ASP.

If Jessica had been taught to read the signs of antisocial personality disorder and trust her instincts, she would not be miserable, lonely and self-doubting, under the influence of an ASP. She would have noticed the coldly amused reaction Amber had to other people's suffering in high school, the pattern of gossip and cruel words, and not seen it as just "normal high school stuff," as Jessica later explained, but as budding antisocial behavior. She would have recognized that setting her up for painful situations by warning Jessica to not be "weird" or "annoying," when entering strange situations, and then abandoning Jessica, were deliberately cruel actions.

Practice being reserved and appropriately humble; coach your children to do likewise.

Being reserved and self-effacing has an undeservedly poor reputation. Our culture praises keeping the world informed of your passing whims via tweets, posts, and status updates. Modesty is often confused with some sort of 19th-century, faux-Victorian way of behaving. While introversion is much more than being reserved, we must keep in mind that as a natural state, extroversion is not a compelling reason to be brash and attention-seeking. The myth has conflated being outgoing with being an attention-seeking black hole, drawing in all possible sensations and validation.

The societal effects of so many people bragging is evidenced by the link between time spent in social media and increased risk of depression. Inflated, fake projections in social media can trick us into believing that our real lives, and real selves, are insufficient. In reality, the ones who seem to thrive online are exhibitionists and those who are more comfortable with dishonesty. It is also a venue where bullying, harassment and cruelty thrive. Minimize exposure to what is a safe haven for ASPs.

Stop apologizing for your natural disposition and figure out how to use it for good.

Surprisingly, many people really don't know what their natural disposition is. In the United States, about 1/3 of the population skews towards introversion, and about 2/3 towards extroversion. The differences have biological roots; introverts' brains and extroverts' brains are different. The higher activity level inside introverts' skulls means less external stimulation is required to reach an optimal level. Extroverts, on the other hand, crave more external stimulation in order to reach their optimal level of arousal. The differences will affect what is considered exhausting and what is considered refreshing. Brief questionnaires based on the Myers-Briggs Type test can give you a basic assessment. The more expensive and thorough Myers-Briggs Type Indicator (MBTI) is an excellent source of understanding. The MBTI is based on substantial research and Carl Jung's theories, and has been used for decades to identify personal styles and strengths.

Introverts may be labelling themselves as "socially awkward," when they are not awkward at all. They merely have a sensitive social barometer. Introverts often have to learn to compensate and function in a world that demands much interaction, but then must be prepared to take the time to refuel. For introverts, this usually means quiet time, alone or with one or two companions, to process what's been happening, reflect, and recuperate. The introverted professor, for example, will be able to interact well with students and colleagues, and require some quiet work time. Her extroverted counterpart will want more social interaction, leaving the quiet desk work more often to stroll around in search in interaction and an injection of energy.

Extroverts need to adapt to a world that, for all its bias in favor of the outgoing, also demands times of quiet, reflection and self-control. The stimulation-seeking extrovert will need to learn to adapt to the quiet aspects of work, study, and prayer. These are often a challenge to the extrovert's natural need for external stimulation. An extroverted student may find it easier to study with music, or in a study group. Adjusting situations to one's general disposition and capitalizing on its strengths, rather than fighting it, can make life easier.

INNIEs and ASPs only appear the same to the uninformed observer. By being able to discern the difference early, we can increase the opportunity to meet good people and reduce the likelihood of being one more victim of the ASP's superficial charm.

4

Your Opinion is as Good as Anyone Else's

SOME OF OUR POPULAR myths started out with very good intentions. The emphasis on encouraging children to have good self-esteem blossomed to new heights in the 1970s. Adults were passionate about affirming young people's gifts, talents and individual qualities. This is a good thing, since we want children to be secure and happy, healthy and confident. Children deserve to feel safe and secure. Every child should know what it is to be loved with tender and protective familial affection; it is the cornerstone of a healthy psyche.

However, out of this enthusiasm for affirmation grew a festering problem. Adults were so eager to affirm children and their uniqueness that praise was slopped about rather indiscriminately. Teachers graded for effort rather than performance; athletes won ribbons for showing up, not winning. Long before everyone was given a trophy for attending a soccer tourney, though, a particularly dangerous myth arose: that oft-repeated line, "Your opinion is as good as anyone else's."

Your Opinion is as Good as Anyone Else's

Parents say it to their children; friends reassure one another. The plethora of blogs and opinion posts make it seem that merely asserting that something is an "opinion" renders it attention-worthy and on par with other opinions. An only mildly less toxic version asserts that we all "have a right to our opinions," without linking that right to the responsibility of enduring the consequences of that opinion.

What happens when we teach children, with rigor and repetition, that their opinions are as good as anyone else's?

> *Christopher is preparing for Confirmation. An 8th grader in a parochial school, the past two years of religious education have focused on not only educating him about his faith but helping him prepare to be an adult member of the congregation. It's not merely education; it's a time of formation, of adapting one's interior life, mental structures and spiritual compass to the highest principles. He is expected to engage fully in the formation process: not one merely of memorizing facts, but one of integrating the material into his way of discerning and acting. Christopher's task is to begin to think, feel and behave like an active, dynamic young Catholic adult. Confirmation is only a few months away, and his religion teachers, pastor and sponsor are increasingly aware of a burgeoning problem. Christopher is not open to the notion of formation. Christopher is routinely disrespectful during classes and, when questioned about this, asserts that he doesn't "agree" with some particular rule, teaching, or passage from Scripture. Engaging in dialogue is of little use because Christopher, like many of his friends, has been raised to believe that his opinions are as good as anyone else's. He doesn't like the rules, he thinks they are "stupid," and, since he has been encouraged to believe in the rightness of his opinions, he sees no reason to be swayed by his better-educated superiors. They have their opinion, and he has his, he shrugs. Christopher should not be permitted to participate in the sacrament, as he isn't a sincere candidate.*

For a long time, many in our culture have been encouraging young people to believe that their opinions are as good as anyone else's. It's meant to be empowering, and, like many things that generate power, ought to be managed very carefully. Christopher, the boy preparing for his faith's rite of passage into spiritual responsibility and adulthood, does not have the knowledge to make an informed, useful opinion about his faith, its tenets and traditions. This boy, like many people, has major differences of "opinion" with his faith. The problem is, he has been raised to believe that his opinion is no less significant than centuries of teachings of rabbinical scholars, as well as the wisdom of Augustine, Thomas Aquinas, and subsequent theologians. That he should have to surrender the absolute value of his opinion and attempt to study, learn about, and form his conscience in relation to others, who know more than he, is anathema to him. He seems to think that the Ten Commandments are someone's opinion, or that his faith's teaching on the dignity of human life is part of a "one from column A, one from column B" menu. He is not content to put his opinions aside, and boldly argues with the clergy assigned the unfortunate duty of preparing him for his rite of passage. He isn't just asking thoughtful questions to seek understanding, which would be perfectly reasonable and a sign of healthy engagement. He's asking questions that are designed to block understanding. He is not curious; he is contemptuous.

This child is not unique. People pull opinions out of thin air—or out of popular culture, which is worse—and make decisions based on their current emotional state. If they were honest, they'd admit they are most often deciding things based on raw emotions at best. Most people don't want to hear about forming their conscience; they confuse their conscience with their emotions, and emotions with instincts. When people confuse instincts with a conscience, bad things happen. "I feel this way so it must make sense," is a very dangerous heuristic. The psychological term is emotional reasoning, and it's considered an irrational pattern of thinking.

Emotional reasoning is amenable to reformatting via personal discipline. It can be addressed in a very straightforward, practical way in cognitive-behavioral approaches to psychotherapy. Success in this endeavor depends upon whether the person is willing to question the validity of the emotionally-charged reactions trying to pass themselves off as logical opinions.

We have a double corruption: the corruption of the definition, and the corruption of integrity and education. At one level, the problem begins with the corruption of the word, opinion. Opinions are mental judgments, formed deliberately, and often are the province of experts or judges. The underlying premise of an opinion is that knowledge is considered in its development. An opinion is not a whim, or a feeling, or a random notion tossed out to keep the conversation limping along. The myth doesn't tend to work out well for the true believers in opinion-equity. When Christopher's parents began their drumbeat strain of, "Your opinion is as good as anyone else's," they did not anticipate his being rude to the parish priest or insulting beloved Aunt Mary, his erstwhile Confirmation sponsor, who was so pleased, initially, to be invited to share this spiritual journey with Christopher. Christopher is not on a journey. He is putting in his time and looking forward to it being "done." His parents thought they were encouraging him to have good self-esteem and self-confidence. They didn't want him to grow up abashed and diffident. They worried that he would be bullied, just take whatever others might deal out to him or acquiesce to peer pressure. They hoped, desperately, that he would be confident enough in his own thinking to stick to his principles and not do anything self-destructive and foolish. These are realistic concerns, and it makes sense that parents want to give children the tools they will need to survive their social world. Like most parents, though, Christopher's mom and dad did not understand that to the concrete, literal mind of a child the words will mean precisely what they say. He will not wrestle with whether or not it applies across contexts. It was not modified and made conditional by the adults, so it will certainly not be adapted by Christopher.

The second part of the corruption involves the devolution of education. Critical thinking and humility, two essential factors in learning and maturation, are given short shrift. Critical thinking is often dumbed down to mere ill-informed criticizing. This can be seen in, among other places, creative arts classes. Often in secondary school or college, the class begins with a critique period. Students asked to engage in a critique often start out with clumsy, negative comments on one another's work. They believe this is what the professor wants: you want a critique, right? Isn't that the same as criticism?

> Two weeks into the term, Alicia dreads the first fifteen minutes of her painting class. They line up their work and the instructor facilitates a critique period. It seems like open season on everyone's confidence: two of the brasher, outgoing students are all too eager to chime in with negative comments. "I don't like that yellow you used on the cliff face," Robert asserts loudly. Jennifer chimes in with a similar sentiment. Before Alicia can respond, though, the instructor injects a question, this time for Robert and Jennifer. "This isn't about what you like or don't like," Ms. Allen says. "Robert and Jennifer, why don't you each explain the rationale for your comment and have a dialogue with Alicia about her intentions, the reasons for her choice, and the reasons you might have chosen differently?" For once, the loquacious Robert and Jennifer are at a loss for words. Looking a bit peeved, Robert mumbles something about his opinion, and not having to explain it. "It's just my opinion." Ms. Allen smiles gently and replies, "No, Robert, the whole point of critique is to explain and support your opinion and enter into a conversation about the various choices in a given situation and the reasons for and against each. Saying you like, or don't like, someone's work is not an opinion, not without more explanation." The class is quiet, with lots of shifting of feet and eyes. The rest of the critique period is subdued. Soon they are working at their easels. For most of the class, next week's critique has become far less intimidating.

Of course, true criticism is not merely disparagement. A critique is an attempt to enter the mindset of the creator, to view the work and the intentions, and to make thoughtful observations on the aspects of the work that do, and do not, seem to promote the artist's intentions. Viewing a fellow student's landscape and

Your Opinion is as Good as Anyone Else's

remarking callously that, "I don't like those yellow brush strokes on the cliff face over there," is not a critique. It's not even a real opinion; it's just an emotional response disguised as a thought. To kindly say, "I see that the yellow strokes are meant to indicate the tones of late-day sunlight, and I wonder if perhaps a warmer shade of yellow would have served better," is a thoughtful opinion, a critique, and invites discussion and growth in understanding. The artist whose work is being critiqued can hear, in the insightful comment, an understanding of the difference in quality of light at different times of day as well as the use of different temperatures of color to create these nuances. The artist can infer a certain degree of expertise within the offered opinion, which makes the feedback useful and meaningful.

We have spent so much time telling children that their opinion is as good as anyone else's, without regard to knowledge, expertise, or wisdom, that we now have two generations of adults, and another en route, who don't believe that differences in opinion between themselves and experts are of any significance whatsoever. This problem rears its head in professional preparation programs. For example, graduate students have to be told—repeatedly—that they should either not have opinions or understand that their opinions are irrelevant. They don't know enough to have an opinion on the information at hand, not until well into their training and even then, they should be pointing back to science. It's a hard sell, in a world that values cockiness over actual accomplishment and belligerence over deference. Consider, for example, the inherent challenge for modern students in this assignment:

> Assignment: select one mental disorder diagnosis from the current American Psychiatric Association manual. Briefly describe the main symptoms. Describe, compare and contrast two treatments for this disorder drawn from the peer-reviewed literature less than three years old.

There is little space in this assignment, if any, for personal opinion, yet a significant plurality of my students feel inclined to share their opinions about the diagnostic criteria, the various treatments, and offer anecdotal evidence (the experiences of a family member or friend) as a substitute for the required scholarly sources. It is, from my years of experience, impossible to present this simple college assignment in such a way as to avoid numerous submissions being infected with personal anecdotes and ill-formed opinions offered by a student as the appropriate counters to a scholarly research article. Students often conflate their misunderstandings, anecdotes and ill-informed beliefs into a position they believe is interchangeable with empirical data and professional expertise. The confidence in one's assertions as being worthy of analysis in contrast to professional expertise exceeds the developmentally normal slight over-confidence of adolescence. *Counseling Today* (published by the American Counseling Association) supports the suspicion drawn from the anecdotal reports of therapy and education professionals: the incidence of both histrionic personality disorder and narcissistic personality disorder are markedly higher in young adults now than in prior generations. The difference is significant: while a normal distribution of these disorders might be 1 to 3%, the study cited a rate of histrionic personality disorder over 29%, and narcissistic personality disorder at over 21%. Histrionic personality disorder is characterized by constantly demanding attention, being dramatic, self-absorbed, and vain. Narcissistic personality disorder comprises an inflated sense of ability and entitlement, arrogance, and the belief that one deserves to be treated as special and to be surrounded by other, special people. While people who meet these criteria can initially be quite charming and even seductive, the appeal thins when the endless, gaping need for praise and attention becomes apparent. Such people, naturally, believe that their opinions are as good as—if not better than—others'.

Because people who are not narcissistic or histrionic have not been educated to understand precisely what an opinion is, they frequently believe they have lots of thoughtful opinions when in reality they have a lot of feelings, whims, preferences, and wishes, wearing "opinion" like a child playing dress-up in the parent's closet. A preschooler wearing Mama's high heels is adorable, but is not a grown woman; calling a whim an opinion does not make

Your Opinion is as Good as Anyone Else's

it a serious proposition resting on deep understanding of the topic at hand. To large extent, what masquerades as opinion is nothing more than emotional reasoning, the logical error in which someone experiences an emotional state and decides that the situation (whatever it may be) warrants such an emotional response. The emotional reaction is prejudged as outweighing any other data.

Epictetus, Aquinas, and many others recognized this faulty pattern before psychotherapists labeled it one type of irrational thinking and developed specific interventions to counter it. Mental health professionals can help people overcome this error in thinking, particularly with the various forms of cognitive therapy. These are the approaches to psychotherapy most supported by research. They include cognitive-behavioral therapy (CBT) and its cousins, Rational Emotive Behavior Therapy (REBT) and Acceptance and Commitment Therapy (ACT). These cognition-focused forms of therapy work on changing emotions by dealing with the underlying thoughts—whether you call them beliefs, assumptions, expectations, hopes, ideas, or wishes. This approach works for a variety of complaints: depression, anxiety, panic, phobias, relationship problems, even post-traumatic stress disorder. A primary problem is that the process requires we learn to be brutally honest about our thoughts and accept responsibility for the portion of emotion drawn from those thoughts. It also requires the humility to admit that perhaps our opinions are not as right as we would like to think. This clinging to our thoughts, even when they create emotional chaos, is a significant barrier to psychological healing.

> Ben suffers from what psychotherapists describe as social anxiety. He isn't just a little shy; he suffers intense thoughts, feelings and physical symptoms of stress before, during and after social interactions, worrying about what to do or say, and then repeatedly worrying that he said, or did, the wrong things. In desperation, he seeks therapy. The therapist encourages Ben to verbalize, and write down, the particular thoughts that rise up during his times of anxiety. The next step is to begin challenging those thoughts, testing them for accuracy and then developing replacement thoughts, which can be rehearsed until those new

Toxic Mythology

> thoughts become the default paths in the brain and the old, worried patterns fall into decay. The first problem is Ben's shame at being so anxious and clumsy about social settings where everyone else knows what to do (perhaps the first irrational thought to be challenged in therapy!). Another problem, though, is Ben's unwillingness to let go of his ideas. They hurt him, but they make sense to him. He wants to feel better, but feeling better means he will have to admit his old way of thinking was in error, and then endure repeated rehearsals of new ideas that sound good but don't "fit" at first.

Very often clients have healthy ambivalence: they want to be honest, but they have difficulty trusting the therapist too quickly. They fear having their worst fear confirmed: that they are "crazy," whatever they mean by that. On the other hand, they don't want to be tricked or manipulated into thinking, or being, something too different. After all, they have been conditioned to believe that no one's opinions are better than anyone else's . . . so, the thoughts offered for analysis in therapy are, at first, often the most superficial. The client may not be aware of the lie of omission—of failing to reveal the deeper thoughts. The clinician may, likewise, be unaware that the supposed problem thought is just the tip of the iceberg. The client who is stricken with panic attacks before the annual performance review verbalizes being afraid of getting a mediocre review—but dig deeper and you may very well find subterranean fears of being found lacking, fired, burning through savings, and ending up jobless, friendless and homeless. This is an abiding, existential fear that encompasses survival, safety, love and belonging—basic human needs. The panic attacks will be best alleviated by exploring the whole downward spiral of fear-inducing thoughts, learning to reality-test them, challenge them, and then both develop and rehearse believable alternatives that help panic dwindle to a little healthy anxiety, just the amount of mild edge needed to spur effort and commitment to excellence without tipping over into dread and despair.

Overall, it is not complicated to work through how your thinking undermines your emotional well-being. It does require that you be able to verbalize your thoughts. However, if you are married to your ideas (in the old fashioned, 'til-death-do-us-part sense) you will have incredible difficulty imagining that your thoughts are less than documented facts. They may actually be open to debate, or possibly wrong. Even silly. Sometimes wrong thinking is an old habit—a way of seeing things that one should have outgrown, like worrying about being "cool" or fretting about whether anyone will ask you to the prom. In these cases, gradually rehearsing new ways of thinking can supersede old thinking and change the emotions that go with those old thoughts.

Being enamored of your emotions and naming them opinions entails many risks. People vote based on emotion rather than any sense of constitutional law, history or world events. They marry based on hanging out and having fun with no knowledge of one another's real character or life goals. They parent based on fear of disapproval, and are lorded over by their offspring. It means that one mistakes a passing psychological or physiological itch for hate or love.

It may mean failure to develop a conscience worthy of anyone over the age of seven. Seven, of course, used to be considered the age of reason but I am not sure. When teenagers believe that they have as much right to assert right and wrong as experts in Mosaic Law or the Roman Catholic Church, it may be that potentially reasonable seven year olds devolve into instinct-driven narcissists. Or it may be that two generations of "Your opinion is worth as much as anyone else's," has come home to roost.

THE ANTIDOTES:

Unfortunately, separating wishes and preferences from logical opinions will be difficult for many people. Much of it involves creating new habits, which can take a month or so of dedication. Here are some simple strategies to get started. You'll notice that most of these will work with children, too.

Toxic Mythology

Banish the term, "Your opinion is as good as anyone else's," from your vocabulary. It isn't true, so stop lying to yourself and to the people you love.

Asking people to explain their opinion, if done respectfully, can increase understanding for you and for the opinion-holder. For example, if Alicia had not learned through unpleasant experiences to dread interaction with Robert in art class, she might have asked him, politely and genuinely, why he disapproves of the yellow she used on the cliff faces in her landscape. If Robert has an opinion (instead of a preference dressed up in opinion-clothing), he will be able to explain it, and a helpful conversation can ensue. If Robert has no basis for his opinion, then it's not an opinion. It's personal taste, or a whim, and Robert has every right to his personal tastes in art. Those, however, are not expert opinions.

This is a helpful exercise with children. Instead of encouraging them to verbalize their own opinions, model the process of supporting an opinion with factual information. Children may not be fans of this process, but they will certainly learn from it:

> "I don't want to go to bed at 8:30. My friends get to stay up later," argues your ten-year-old. "Well, you may not want to go to bed, but you're going to your room at 8:30," you respond. "Why?" demands your child. You can respond in lots of ways, but this time you say, "Well, it's better for you than staying up late." "That's just your opinion!" your child replies. Instead of being defensive or raising the stakes, this time you take a calming breath and say, "You're right, it is my opinion. It took a while to learn enough to make an opinion about this. I wasn't sure what the best thing was for you. So, I read some doctors' articles on what is best for kids' brains and bodies, and it seems that the experts have proven that getting a nice, long night's sleep is better than staying up late." "Well, it's not my opinion," says your child. "I know," you say, "But, honey, you don't know enough about this to have a real opinion. You're saying opinion, but we both know you mean you just really, really want to stay up as late as your friends, no matter what some

Your Opinion is as Good as Anyone Else's

doctor says. I know you think it would be more fun to stay up later, but that's not the same as an opinion."

You won't get happy faces, but don't be surprised if, before long, you hear your child instructing a sibling or friend about something not being an opinion because it's not based on knowing about stuff, it's just what the other child wants.

Generate a list of words to replace "opinion" and practice using them when they are more appropriate. Preference, wish, idea, thought, desire—these are all beautiful words and mean very different things. Instead of using "opinion" as a go-to term, substitute one of these.

Notice how you feel about it. Do you feel weak if you don't assert an opinion? We've been conditioned to believe we have to assert ourselves, and our opinions. To fail to do so is to be weak, passive, a pushover. However, often we are talking about matters of taste. Sometimes, of course, we have the happy intersection of our preferences and our expertise. In these cases, an enthusiastic and well-informed opinion can be interesting and useful. If you have been using assertions of opinion as a way to appear confident, knowledgeable and firm, stepping back from this position can feel weak and vulnerable. Without the shield of an opinion, you may wonder if others will attack you, question you, or override your preferences. The myth, your opinion is as good as anyone else's, has an equally dark shadow: failure to assert your opinion is a sign of weakness and passivity. Reflecting on the degree to which this underbelly of the myth poisons your interactions is a worthwhile endeavor. After all, if it is true that "your opinions are as good as anyone else's" then failing to have one is a sign of weakness, of some strange mental anemia.

If failing to provide an opinion does create feelings of anxiety, it's helpful to reflect on the underlying fears. Remember the discussion of emotional reasoning? Simply because not having an opinion feels unsettling doesn't mean it is an unsafe position.

Toxic Mythology

Notice the automatic thoughts that are related to the unease. "She'll think I'm stupid," or, "He'll assume I'm ignorant," are typical. These thoughts warrant some exploration and questioning.

> *What makes you believe she will think you are stupid for not having an opinion?*
> *So what if she thinks you are stupid?*
> *Does her thinking you so mean that you are stupid?*
> *Does failing to assert an opinion based on little, or no, information seem smarter than withholding judgment?*
> *So what if he thinks you are ignorant?*
> *What if you are ignorant on this topic? Is that necessarily a problem? Are there topics about which you'd rather be ignorant? Professional criminal practices and certain paraphilia are often within the domain of things about which many people would prefer to retain ignorance.*

In reality, letting go of the need to have an opinion is intensely freeing. Without the shield of false expertise and a position to defend, one can be open to absorbing information, thinking critically, and have the pleasure of developing a real, informed opinion if you choose to invest the energy. The dishonest myth, that all opinions are of equal value, serves the dark impulse that keeps us apart by feeding pride and its shadow, insecurity. You will enjoy the psychological benefit of not using mental energy better invested elsewhere in frantically maintaining a smokescreen of false confidence and expertise. People can usually tell when we are dishonest, and pretending to have expertise is a subtle form of dishonesty. Being our genuine, far-from-all-knowing, selves means having a chance at authentic relationships.

Look for opportunities to defer having an opinion.

When asked about something about which you don't have much information, or expertise, say, "I don't know enough about that to really have an opinion. What are your thoughts about it?" Again, notice how you feel about making such a statement. Feelings of

Your Opinion is as Good as Anyone Else's

anxiety indicate you have been using "opinions" as a way to fend off the world. Opinions are inadequate armor.

Admitting you don't know enough to have an opinion, and inviting input, can be an excellent strategy to use with children. When a child asserts an "opinion," seek understanding. Ask about the rationale for the opinion. If, for example, your teenager asserts that anyone can see that Dali was a much more significant artist than Caravaggio, you have a golden opportunity to scout out the rationale. Is this knowledgeable art criticism, which would make it an opinion? Is the child parroting a favorite teacher's opinion, with a bit of understanding, which is the beginning of reliance on expertise to form opinion? Is it simply a preference in style and subject? That makes it a matter of taste, not opinion. Be wary of seeming to attack. Be genuinely curious and respectful. This models the reasonable behavior you'd like in return. Expect some defensiveness and resistance when you ask in an attempt to understand, because odds are, your child has done very well at absorbing the myth that all opinions are created equal. If you find the child can't defend the opinion, suggest that the two of you look into this issue together, or separately, and then revisit it. Even if the child drops the ball, follow up on it; it shows you were really open to ideas, not merely playing games with the child's ego.

> *Remember when we went to the museum and we wondered which artist was more influential, Dali or Caravaggio? Well, I followed up by looking up a few art history sites and I found that . . .*

Don't be disappointed if every attempt to bridge preferences with opinions isn't met with enthusiasm, but be persistent. You are modeling humility, curiosity, respect and intellectual flexibility, and those are going to be much more useful than a mistaken belief that "my opinion is as good as anyone else's."

5

Money Can't Buy Happiness, or Can It?

"You can't buy happiness," the saying goes. Conversely, the field of happiness economics points to positive correlations between nations' GDP and the population's happiness across various measures. Apparently, the myth about money and happiness works both ways. Money cannot buy happiness; money can buy happiness. In reality, of course, money impacts happiness. However, even this expression is muddy. What do we mean by "happiness?" What do we mean by "money?"

In psychology, we look at the emotional world in terms of *states* and *traits*. An emotional state is often referred to as a feeling; it is by definition transient. You're feeling relaxed now; a sudden noise outside will have you startled; when you determine that it was merely a raccoon trying to break into the trash can, you will have feelings of relief and annoyance. Those rapidly shifting feelings are emotional states. It is, in a sense, the melody line of the emotional world.

A trait is something different; it is enduring and stable. The steady bass line of the emotional world, a trait is more of a characteristic rather than an experience. Consider, for example, the

Money Can't Buy Happiness, or Can It?

reader startled by what turns out to be a mischievous raccoon trying to steal trash. The emotionally calm (trait) reader will rapidly resettle in a relaxed mode, immersed once more in reading. An emotionally anxious (trait) reader will have difficulty settling down from the startled mode; naturally a bit edgy and high strung, the anxious reader will be preoccupied with other, anxiety-provoking thoughts. Aroused to worry, the reader wanders mentally from the book, to whether the side door is locked, to the health of a friend. This is a very different way of being than naturally defaulting—as a trait—to serenity. Of course, these traits are on a continuum, with stoicism on one end and full-blown neurosis (common to characters in a Woody Allen film) on the other.

If we consider happiness as a trait, rather than a transient state, then we see that it is not the same as "having fun," or being entertained. Having fun, or excitement, is a chemical rush of dopamine, the "feel good" neurotransmitter. It's a flash of thrill. It is not the enduring experience of real happiness. The trait of happiness includes a sense of hopefulness; it is a kind of contentment mixed with appreciation for the past and anticipation of the future. Happiness makes space for intense joy and quiet serenity. Being a happy person does not preclude sadness, or anxiety, or anger. Those are natural, normal emotions and belong in the texture of life. For a happy person, though, those negative emotions are perceived as not the defining theme but rather as elements in a larger picture.

This is a position supported by faith traditions and Scripture as well as by the growing discipline and science of Positive Psychology. Positive Psychology focuses on strengths such as resiliency, compassion, and the ability to connect deeply with others. The same traits resonate within a Judeo-Christian understanding of the nature of happiness.

Resiliency is the capacity to bounce back from adversity. Challenges and difficulties are inescapable, but some people seem to find ways to survive and even thrive in difficult times. Surprisingly, resiliency is not merely some natural gift—you've got it, or you don't—but a set of mental skills that can be deliberately developed. Many scientists, such as the late Al Siebert, Ph.D., have done substantial work in researching and then teaching the skills that comprise resiliency. These skills include maintaining a sense of humor, nurturing one's optimism, and refusing to yield to a "victim" mindset. Not merely aspects of resiliency, these assets are also ingredients in happiness.

> Melissa, along with ten other people, lost their jobs when the local hardware store closed. Unemployment benefits were small, and all eleven were searching for work in an area already hit hard by the recession. Melissa allowed herself a couple of days of what she referred to as a pity party, and then swung into action. She started volunteering to make sandwiches for the homeless outreach program at her church; she figured, she wasn't doing anything most Tuesday afternoons, anyway. She let other people know she'd been laid off and was actively looking for work. She contacted her former coworkers and invited them to her house for a bring-your-own-lunch get together on a regular basis; she didn't think sitting at home alone all day, every day, was good for her or anyone else. A few showed up; most of them did not. Melissa kept applying for jobs, reapplying at the same companies every month or so when openings were posted in the papers or online. She found a job in four months. A year later, she ran into one of her coworkers, Tom, for the first time since the layoff. Tom had been on unemployment the entire year, and seemed angry and depressed. Tom immediately began complaining about what their former employer had "done to us," and Melissa realized that Tom was stuck. For Tom, it was as if the layoff had just happened. He was in a kind of miserable stasis.

Melissa had, without realizing it, embraced basic principles for happiness. She had reached out in service to others, maintained social connections, persevered in her job search, and tried her best to maintain a positive attitude. Note that for the first four months, she and Tom had the same situation, in terms of money. Yet, within a few days of the layoff, their reports of personal happiness would have already been far different.

Money Can't Buy Happiness, or Can It?

Melissa was able to tap into her personal strengths, feel compassion for others despite her own difficulties, and worked to build and maintain social connections. These are essential for happiness and don't directly cost us anything.

Compassion, being able to share in the sufferings and joys of others, is one of the traits emphasized in Positive Psychology and intrinsic to Judeo-Christian faith traditions. It may seem contradictory that sharing someone's sorrow has something to do with the capacity for happiness, but both actions have much to do with being outside of oneself, rather than preoccupied with the spinning worries in one's head. If we bear in mind that happiness has less to do with momentary twinges of good feelings and hiccups of dopamine than with a pervasive sense of hopefulness and emotional well-being, then an appreciation of the good, and the bad, of life, can fit within that experience.

Connection with others at an emotional level is essential for happiness. While one person may thrive with one deep, rich relationship and another person prefers many relationships that meet different emotional and social needs, the need for at least one human relationship is well-supported by research. We see in our current society a tendency to have multiple shallow and often artificial relationships, based on electronic interactions and a sharing of day-to-day details of life or a glamorized presentation of one's life. This may make the relationship more harmful than helpful. Research indicates that more "friends" on social media correlates to a higher risk for depression, due in large part to endless comparison with others' online presentations.

The Judeo-Christian view of the meaningful life, of course, is transcendent. We worship an imminent and engaged Deity but also look at this passing world as a place in which to find meaning and purpose. Resiliency corresponds to the virtue of hope; compassion and connection to the virtue of charity. The person who is living in openness to graces and attempting to live out these virtues ought to be, ideally, a trait-happy person. Unhappiness may be a passing state, or something requiring attention and assistance, as in depression, grief or despair.

Money is, strangely, also hard to define. Money is not merely a big pile of coins. Money is the means to obtain things we need and want. In another time, we may have bartered (I will trade you a loaf of bread for some eggs; I will care for your children while you go fishing if you will share some fish with me). The Internal Revenue Service frowns on this process, and so we resort to using money as a physical symbol of time and effort. Money is worth only as much as it will buy.

Research has repeatedly indicated a certain amount of financial security and material comfort lends itself towards greater emotional fulfillment. Money is the means, in our culture, of obtaining material security. We need look no further than Psychology 101 and everyone's first introduction to Maslow's Hierarchy of Needs. Maslow and his colleagues in the Humanistic Psychology movement were revolutionaries. To appreciate how radical Maslow was, consider the roots of psychology.

As a separate field of research, psychology was born in the second half of the 19th century. This was a time in which major cultural shifts were underway. It was the age of Darwin, Marx and Nietzsche. The intellectuals of the time were largely moving away from traditional Judeo-Christian values. For its part, in the late 19th century, psychology was focused on the nature of consciousness. Researchers sought to understand both the process and function of consciousness and thought. Freud, a neurologist and researcher, posited that unconscious conflicts between our instinctive drives and the mores of society created psychological problems. The theory tended to emphasize that while our instincts are natural, emotional problems arise primarily from the conflicting demands of society. The trend to devalue traditional ethics and Judeo-Christian morality was pervasive. Western nations attacked religion. France nationalized church properties in 1905. Mexico essentially banned the practice of Catholicism in 1926. Hitler's National Socialist government took over the Lutheran Church in the 1930s, leading to the development of the rebellious and illegal "Confessing Church," whose leaders included martyred theologian Dietrich Bonhoeffer.

Darwin's theory of the gradual change of particular species over time, based on adapting to the environment, was hijacked by philosophers of an atheistic bent. A corrupted version of Darwin's theory became social Darwinism, in which "survival of the fittest" was not about the gradual improvement of a species but rather about the need, and right, of the "fittest" humans to dominate, and subsequently the devaluing of those deemed less "fit." By the 1920s, social Darwinism's brutal fruits were already appearing in the United States' eugenics movement. Germany adopted this philosophy as an excuse to begin the extermination of mentally ill and intellectually handicapped people (using a poison gas, as George Bernard Shaw had suggested in 1910). Also in the 1920s, psychology began shifting to be more scientific: behaviorism became a means for psychology to be taken seriously, like the hard sciences that were making so much progress. At its most extreme, behaviorism completely discounted the interior life; what could not be measured was irrelevant. Humans were automatons, to be conditioned—manipulated—as their masters or managers saw fit.

When World War II was over, and the entire world was faced with the unspeakable consequences of diminishing people to mere biology, theorists such as Frankl, Rogers and Maslow came forth in what was eventually seen as a third option in psychology. This school of thought, the Humanistic movement of psychology, was something new; it did not see people as merely soulless animals to be manipulated externally as the behaviorists asserted, nor did the humanistic school see humans as haplessly driven by instincts and unconscious conflicts. While Jung injected spirituality into psychoanalytic theory (as did others), the original humanistic movement embraced the transcendent and meaning-seeking nature of humanity.

Maslow was a primary figure in the development of this still-extant area of psychology. He postulated a hierarchy of needs, usually represented as a pyramid. The more basic needs such as survival and safety, are at the bottom. Next comes the need for love and belonging; then the need for esteem, meaning to feel valued and to have a sense of one's own value. Often this is met via meaningful work and service. Finally, the top level is self-actualization, which comprises intense spiritual experiences, openness and creativity, and an abiding sense of meaning and joy. As lower needs are met, people progress upwards. People who are preoccupied with survival do not have the luxury of sitting around thinking about their deeply gratifying connections with others. I spent nearly five years working with the indigent, severely mentally ill population. People who are sleeping in shifts under park benches with a buddy sitting guard to avoid being beaten to death or cut up for fun by marauding youth are not worried about happiness. They are hoping to see morning. Happiness will wait.

At the same time, merely having sufficient funds for safety and security is not a guarantee of happiness.

> Enough money to buy security doesn't necessarily bring security. Gabriel is 59. A tremendous financial success, he has two homes: one on a SoCal beach, the other in the Adirondacks. He has a lovely wife, few health problems, and four grown daughters with good husbands, and a few grandchildren to spoil. Semi-retired and enjoying the consultant lifestyle of sharing his expertise, Gabriel "should be" happy. He is not. While he has the bottom layers of Maslow's pyramid as solid as they can be, with his basic needs met and then some, Gabriel is incredibly lonely. Despite the big, happy family, and plenty of friends, Gabriel has been highly competitive for so long that he cannot let down his guard. His deep need to feel loved is buried. The sense that he belongs, as if he really fits in, is . . . wobbly. Doing less feels like being less; he has always made up for insecurity in relationships by doing more/fixing more/being more. He cannot adjust to the slower pace of this stage of life. Instead of relishing the opportunity for exploration, creativity and relatedness, he feels edgy. Settling down feels like settling, like accepting being "less" although when asked "less than what?" he can't give a clear answer. The pain in his eyes at the question, though, is very clear.

As can be seen, not every unhappy person is directly preoccupied with literal survival needs. Research out of Princeton University in 2010 indicated that about $75K/year seemed, at that time,

Money Can't Buy Happiness, or Can It?

to be the income level correlated to maximal happiness. After that, people are not more emotionally happy but indicate they are more satisfied with the "direction" their life is going. I infer from this that they believe, somehow, their lives will be substantially better when they have the means to buy more, or better, stuff. Alternately, it is the comparison to others. They will be happy when they are able to have (buy) a better house/television/car/sex partner than the neighbor. This is a recipe for unhappiness because, of course, someone else will always seem to have outdone you in one way or another. Covetousness is a major sin because it poisons humans from the inside out, and erodes relationships. Placed in the context of Maslow's pyramid of needs, a chronically covetous person cannot truly meet anything but survival and safety. Love and belonging will be constantly tainted by envy and pride, and the needless comparison of self-to-others will undercut healthy esteem.

Of course, a sizeable slice of our culture is based on retail therapy. Pick up almost any magazine aimed at women, and you will find two primary themes: articles that point out what is lacking in you (or your life), and advertisements for products to remedy those deficiencies. Television and computer sites saturate us with advertisements, often tailored to our particular browsing habits. I once read up on a car a family member was interested in purchasing and was barraged with advertisements for it each time I was online for weeks. Certainly the happy, healthy, confidently smiling people we see in advertisements seem to have what we all crave: an interior state that has little, if anything, to do with what they are selling. Enough money to buy the good stuff doesn't guarantee happiness.

> *Melissa is chronically unhappy, and has been feeding this with what she jokingly refers to as "retail therapy." She reports to her therapist that she has an entire closet full of sheet sets, still in the original packaging. She buys new closet organization systems, new handbags and totes, and imagines that she will be "different" when she has these things. The organization system will make it possible to put her house in order, but, of course, it doesn't; it can't. The "house" that is out of order for Melissa is emotional.*

Toxic Mythology

> *Her deep unhappiness with her life, her lack of human connection and purpose, are floundering in a desire to impose order and buy things that promise a fresh start.*

The person who is disorganized will not magically be serene and uncluttered with the right home-storage system; the person unhappily fighting through rush hour traffic will not be happily grooving to smooth jazz in stop and go traffic in a more expensive car. A person's interior states will not be significantly altered by more expensive accoutrements.

Other studies have indicated a magic annual income number somewhat lower than $75K, but the message is the same. When basic survival and security needs are met, people are able to actually be in their lives rather than doggy-paddling desperately to keep themselves, and their possessions, afloat. The new economy, of course, makes this a bigger challenge. Working 50 hours a week is not a terrible cross to bear. If it is only one job, there are a lot of hours, but only one or two bosses, one source of workplace politics, one schedule, one set of coworkers, one set of customers . . . the mental bandwidth required to cope with the details of the job do not change dramatically between 35 and 50 hours. Many people, though, are now juggling 2, 3 or even 4 part-time jobs. The total hours may still be only 40 to 45 per week, but often, each job carries its own overhead. The person juggling multiple part-time endeavors is keeping track, mentally, of four jobs' worth of rules, details, and politics. Someone working part-time jobs for one grocery chain, a hardware store and one restaurant chain must juggle not just the rules and requirements, but also substantial memorization for each position.

> *Jane fantasizes about . . . having one job. A recent college graduate, she is still at her high school job, waiting tables at a local restaurant. She also works part-time work in her field (mental health), doing telephone intakes at the local mental health clinic. She delivers newspapers in the early morning hours. Her total hours are about 50 hours a week, which isn't bad at all. However, the 3 AM wakeup to load up her papers and start her route, the quick clean-up in the*

Money Can't Buy Happiness, or Can It?

> *rest room before starting her morning job at the clinic, and keeping track of her paper route, the changing menu and the protocols at the clinic keep her mind overflowing. Unless she begs someone she can trust to cover for her on the paper route, she never has a day off. It's wearing her down. She also spends about five hours a week looking for full time work in her field. Her friends, who have "real" jobs, keep inviting her to join them for fun activities but she's so stressed out and busy that she doesn't feel up to joining them. A bike ride, a movie, or dinner at someone's home just feels like one more thing on the "to-do" list.*

Mental capacity is a finite resource, and when it is being utilized for work "stuff," it's unavailable for anything else. The "anything elses" are often the things that really do yield the possibility for happiness: being in the moment and fully experiencing the wonder of nature, the flow of creativity, connection with loved ones. The multi-tasking, exhausted and sleep-deprived have reduced capacity for this in-the-moment, mindful, and potentially joyful state of being.

It is not the money, per se, which buys the happiness, but the security that money affords that yields the physical, mental and emotional space for the pursuit of happiness. We can see this in the case of those who are in religious vocations in which there is on the one hand, a vow of personal poverty and on the other a lack of concern about tomorrow's needs. For the religious sister, brother or the parish priest, while the personal bank account is very small, the needs for food, shelter, transportation and health care are met by the religious community. The worries that haunt the lay person are much reduced, and as a result there is space available for deeper prayer, deeper connection with others, and (we hope) a more profound connection with meaning, purpose and happiness.

On the other hand, of course, having enough money that worry is unnecessary is no guarantee for happiness. Happiness will be pursued by many to no avail. The reasons vary. Sometimes, when people are consumed with measuring what they do not have, there is not sufficient energy left to enjoy what they have. Perhaps they are busy holding onto something that needs letting go. Others

69

have been raised to equate being passively entertained with being happy, and do not understand that happiness requires some sort of effort. Ultimately, though, it can be boiled down to failing to learn the toddler's lesson. The square, circle, oval, and even the star, cannot fit into that heart-shaped hole. Money cannot buy the common sense to only attempt to fill the heart with things that belong in the heart.

> Jody's a "trust fund baby." Fortunate to be born into a wealthy and accomplished family, she has the world on a string . . . except she's bored. With lots of money at her disposal and not much responsibility, she has "friends" with whom she drinks and does drugs . . . as long as she's buying. She lies about being at school, and instead is hanging out with friends, trying to get by on charm and her family connections when found out by family members, teachers or police. Angry at any limits set on her "fun," she is not really happy, but instead rushes from thrill to thrill. She's tried many street drugs, dabbled in all sorts of sexual experimentation, and unabashedly shares private experiences with her "friends" in the online world. At 17, she is not sure what she wants to do with her life except "have fun" and acts annoyed at anyone who presses her for a better answer. For someone who is having so much fun, she's deeply unhappy and avoids being alone, and sober, because that's when reality has a chance to surface.

Without a sense of purpose in her life, except the pursuit of the thrill of any given moment, Jody isn't able to be happy. She can experience good feelings as passing states, have fun, be amused and entertained, but the transcendent escapes her. She attempts to catch it with drugs, and for a short period of time, club drugs that blend hallucinogens with amphetamines (such as Ecstasy) can bring a replica of the enthusiasm and emotional intimacy she craves, but the drugs wear off and she is left with a hangover, creeping brain damage, and the same disengaged, shallow life she had the day before the latest party.

Late in life, Freud, like Maslow, emphasized two important ingredients for happiness: good relationships and meaningful

Money Can't Buy Happiness, or Can It?

work. Humans aspire for a sense of meaning and purpose in life. We find this through our work, whether that work is a job, a passionate avocation or hobby, service to our families or in volunteering, or as students. The importance of purpose becomes manifest when someone loses a job: it's not just the money, it's the sense of having something useful and important to do. Retirees who don't engage in purposeful activities will become depressed, apathetic, or bored. This leads to a shorter life expectancy than their active, engaged counterparts.

A lack of purpose is a recipe for unhappiness. It is easily seen in celebrities who are wealthy and seem to have no sense of purpose beyond entertaining themselves and seeking publicity. Is someone who makes risqué videos for public consumption, goes shopping for fun, abuses drugs and alcohol, or makes a public habit of putting other people down happy? I doubt it; instead, they are creating a whirlwind of sensations to distract themselves from a deep dissatisfaction and an inability to see a simple way forward towards real happiness. They are trying to buy happiness.

So, while we know that money cannot literally buy happiness, there are material things we truly need. When our basic needs are met, or we believe they are met, energy is available to seek upwards, towards the transcendent, where happiness can be finally found. We are easily tempted to try to fill emotional needs with things money can buy. It's also tempting to be too dismissive of basic needs, to criticize ourselves for not appreciating what we have, and distance ourselves from happiness by feeling depressed.

When emotional insecurity masks itself behind greed, material goods become a substitute for relationships and the life of the spirit. Insecure people try to ward off the world and emotional pain via piles of stuff and, like small children, want others to admire them for their latest accomplishments and are crushed when approval is not forthcoming.

THE ANTIDOTES:

Faith and science offer the same antidotes to the toxic mythology about money and happiness. Belief in something bigger than us, service, and strong connections to others are critical. Nurturing our creativity, our intellects, and having a sense of purpose are meaning are also intrinsic parts of happiness.

Practice gratitude.

It's free. It is faith- and science-supported, and accessible for everyone. You can practice these simple steps:

Keep a gratitude diary. It can be as simple as writing down, even if only in a word or two, three things for which you are grateful each day. Turn off the television and music, and sit quietly for just a few moments while you do this. Then read, aloud, what you've just written. Then put it away until tomorrow.

Every day, look someone in the eye and thank them for something specific. Taking the moment to make human contact is important for all of us. The healthy humility of expressing gratitude, person to person, is good for us, too.

Express gratitude in writing. Let people know when you appreciate them.

When you pray, start out with the "thank you for . . ." list before you start in with the "I want/I need/I fear . . ." list. Let a few breaths of quiet pass after your thanks, before you begin with intercessory prayer. The guideline of ACTS: Adoration, Contrition, Thanksgiving, Supplication is a good way to organize prayer.

Reduce exposure to commercialism.

Store windows, kiosk displays, catalogues, and ads in any media exist to make you unhappy with what you have and nurture coveting of something more. You can minimize dissatisfaction with your financial situation by spending less time absorbing messages about what you are don't have. Limit your television time; cancel subscriptions to magazines that only feed insecurity and envy. Stop using shopping as a form of recreation and therapy.

Be generous.

If you want to feel more satisfied with what you have, give something away. You can do this in any number of ways. Here are some starters:

Have a charity budget line and stick with it.

Give away one item for every new thing you buy or receive. It will enhance your appreciation and may make you reluctant to bring home new things. The same rule can apply to children: receiving a gift means giving something away to a charity that helps children and families.

Give of your time and talent.

You'll notice that you can do any of these with children, too. Small children can identify things they are happy about; they can say thank you and draw thank-you notes for the gifts and kindnesses shown them. Children don't need much exposure to advertisements, and children, like adults, can be generous with their time, talent and treasure. Some parents give a little extra allowance with the understanding that the child will tithe to the church, synagogue or a charity of the child's choice.

Money and happiness are enmeshed in myths, from King Midas to the many lottery winners whose lives are ruined within a few years of winning. Within those myths are important truths:

You can't buy happiness.

We have basic needs, and what gratifies one need can't fulfill every other need. The money that buys the food and shelter we need can't replace warm relationships, meaningful work and our need for the transcendent.

A side note about depression:

Depression will, of course, interfere with happiness. Depression comprises about 30 pages in the latest edition of the American Psychiatric Association's Diagnostic manual (DSM-5), and is experienced in a myriad of ways: physical symptoms, anger, sadness, apathy, despair and hopelessness. Once medical problems have been ruled out or treated properly, e.g. thyroid diseases, anemia, and auto-immune disorders, the treatments for depression often involve focusing on how people think, strengthening important relationships, and action: exercise, getting outside of one's head and into the world, doing things.

While the proper diagnosis and treatment of depression is beyond the scope of this chapter, it's a significant factor in unhappiness. The modern lifestyle, with its emphasis on materialism, shallow interpersonal connections, insufficient exercise and sleep, inadequate nutrition but superfluous calories, and the substitution of entertainment and distraction for meaning and joy, is a recipe for depression. There are numerous research-supported approaches to depression, and the best will include lifestyle changes that support happiness and well-being.

Anyone can experience feelings of depression, and most people's lifestyles could benefit from some adjusting in terms of balance. Persistent feelings of sadness and despair merit professional help; be sure the professional you choose encourages you to look at your lifestyle and values, rather than just reduce symptoms.

6

That's My Personal Life
Compartmentalization

"BUT THAT'S MY PERSONAL/PROFESSIONAL *life.*" In the post-industrial age, there has been increasing emphasis on compartmentalization. Life is no longer a seamless garment, in which family, friends, faith and work are smoothly integrated. Modern culture assures us we can compartmentalize, and this has developed into a demand that we separate personal and public life. The toxic results include infringements on freedom of religion, and appalling lapses in behavior by public figures.

One of the most common examples would be the conflict between the personal and public behaviors of President Bill Clinton, and the heated dispute at all levels of society as to whether his affair with Monica Lewinsky, and possible other affairs were personal and therefore irrelevant to any discussion of his professional life and public service, or if it were impossible to separate the man from his behavior. Ancient wisdom points to the indivisible quality of human nature: "You cannot serve two masters. Either you will hate the one and love the other, or you will serve the one and despise the other." (Luke, 16:13)

Toxic Mythology

For most of the history of human civilization, people spent their lives close to the same people, often related by blood and culture. Whether nomads or farmers with small villages of necessary artisans, our ancestors lived in a world in which life was largely transparent. Even the poor lived in the public eye, the fishbowl which modern celebrities bemoan as their fate. Personal and professional lives were integrated and known to all. "Is this not the carpenter's son?" mused Jesus' neighbors, and perhaps the faint odor of scandal that surrounded the early months of Mary and Joseph's marriage was implicit in that snide remark. There was no hiding, no invisibility, and no chance at compartmentalization. The nightmare of being naked in public was, from an existential perspective, daily reality. Every squabble and sin was public.

For most of us, living this way is no longer necessary. We can choose to compartmentalize. The price of privacy is isolation. Humans are skilled at numbing the terror of existential crises, at least temporarily. To accomplish this, they break their lives into organized slices, with some set out attractively on the front porch of their lives, and others buried deep in the basement—out of sight, out of mind, for now. We are tempted to believe the promise of science fiction: parallel lives. If you can be one person in public, and another in private, isn't that the best of both worlds? The double-life seems glamorous in spy movies but spy movies are not real life. Compartmentalizing life in the 21st century is a strange and self-contradictory topic. On the one hand, the myth has for some decades been an excuse for the bad behavior of public figures. According to the myth, an invisible dividing line separates what is public, and therefore fair game, from what is private. Private matters, in this conceptualization of the myth, asserts that what happens in private stays private, unless the sorry fellow invites us along, such as philandering presidential contender Gary Hart, in which case it's all fair game.

On the other hand, a great many people make a show of negating any line between private and public persona. A favorite method: using social media to share all sorts of drivel and drama. Some people are online burlesque artists, artfully disguising

That's My Personal Life

themselves while appearing to self-disclose. Others, of course, are stripping naked in every way, imagining that the rest of the participants are, likewise, authentic and present. It is a wicked and reckless game. The modern view of the myth may propose, then, that there is no division between private and public lives: everything is exposed under glaring light. Life in this conception of the myth has all the deliberately garish gracelessness of a Pearlstein nude.

There are, between these angles of the myth, a desirable place that would have seemed familiar and appropriate to our ancestors. Even in the not-too-distant past, most of life was lived largely in public, and in a geographic area so constrained that life was of necessity a seamless garment. There was no use putting on airs or asserting in the pub how great your children were; everyone knew you, they knew your parents, and they knew your children. The bigger question was whether you'd be able to get one of them to agree to let their daughter marry one of your boys, or if they would trust you in a barter of a few head of sheep for a good milk cow. If you lived in town, every marital disagreement and family spat was overheard; money troubles were known; bad habits were public domain. The modern small-town life offers a possibility of the same seamlessness:

> *Jenny is well-liked by her friends and their families. Even-tempered and cheerful, she integrates into her friends' families and in short order feels at home. She has adapted as well as possible to a reality known to many in her small town: her father is a heavy drinker and her mother has her hands full with a job, a drunken husband and a severely disabled family member requiring around-the-clock care. The best option for Jenny is often to stay off the home radar and join one of her surrogate families, of which she has several. Her capacity for resilience and her methods—natural and yet clever for a child still in elementary school—are supported because the whole neighborhood is aware of the home situation. There are sufficient folks to accommodate Jenny's valiant attempts to cope with reality.*

Everyone knows, or has known, a Jenny. In small town life, a parent's repeated DUIs show up in the local newspaper and thus no one will let that person drive their children anywhere. The parent's public shame could be humiliating for the family but also provides Jenny with the community's support in rising above a difficult situation. Jenny has the opportunity for life to be a seamless garment, in which the tragedy of her father's alcoholism and her mother's noble efforts to take care of many people, are understood. Her mother receives oblique support in the form of knowing that Jenny is safe under the watchful eyes of others when she cannot be caregiver and doting mother simultaneously. Jenny's father gets to lie to himself about what a fine father he is, as his daughter grows and thrives, but his audience at the local bar dwindles over the years. Without realizing it, he becomes merely a laughingstock, an object of derision, even as he postures about his success as an artist and scrapes by as a housepainter, offering on occasion to paint Jenny's friends' mothers' a portrait, " . . . in good taste," he assures, of the mother sitting in martini glass. He is too far gone to see that his offer exceeds irony.

It would be convenient for Jenny's father, Andrew, to have had a bit more compartmentalization, or so it would appear. After all, if he is a good painter, what difference ought it to make if he is crude in his attempts at flirtation with other parents, or neglects his family? Why blur the lines? The simple fact is that the man who fails to show up at the breakfast table and see his child off to school is the same man who fails to follow through with contracted obligations. He is one and the same, and pretending there is some magical difference between the personal and the public will create problems.

For Andrew, there is the inevitable delay between having to face the depth of his troubles. If the first time he showed up for a parent-teacher conference reeking of alcohol there had been a public push-back, and expressions of concern that perhaps he was not the sort of fellow you'd want painting your house with your wife and daughter home, well, it would be embarrassing but perhaps a quicker fix than devolving closer to hitting bottom while the whole town pretended not to notice because his behavior was "personal."

For Andrew's wife, there is shame and loneliness. She is left feeling that complaining and seeking remedy will shame her and her husband. She has been holding onto pride by imagining that most people really don't know how bad their situation is, and as she is buried in duties, she is not able to judge accurately how it appears.

Most sadly, Jenny is forced to find a way to deal with the despair of an alcoholic father and an overworked, depressed mother by relying on friends and neighbors to receive the basic needs of attention and affection.

Compartmentalizing the private and public life of a parent doesn't seem to help anyone in the long view.

For certain professions, compartmentalization is held up as a necessity. In my own profession, for example, it is essential to separate our professional and personal lives. However, separating the private and public, and believing in compartmentalization, are not the same. This is not a matter of angels dancing on the heads of pins. The nuances of separating one's thoughts and feelings and making firm decisions about what actions to take, versus believing that there is some mystical divider that allows no cross-contamination, is leading to all sorts of dilemmas for many people.

One such dilemma is the common misconception that professionals of various stripes do not have real emotions about their work or the people with whom they work—patients, clients, customers. One version of the myth asserts that a true professional doesn't even experience real emotions about clients, so having such feelings is a failure from the start. Many people believe that professional mental health counselors' training allows them to be unaffected by stories of others' terrible experiences. A book about child abuse, a friend not in the field once informed me, wouldn't upset me because of my training. Weary of being told of my supposed magical capacity to be untouched by horror, I have taken to telling people who say such things that it is one of the stupidest things I have ever heard.

Naturally we feel for our clients: we weep, we laugh, we rejoice. The extent to which this is overtly shared with the client is managed with expert insight and ongoing consultation. It varies, for example, with the theoretical leanings of the therapist and the stability of the client. A therapist who leans towards the guarded, blank-slate of the analyst will be less self-disclosing of here-and-now reactions to a client's revelations than a more humanistic or existentialist therapist subscribing to authenticity as a primary device of therapy. A client whose behavior does warrant some guilt, but is now having thoughts of suicide due to a pathological level of guilt and self-recrimination, needs comfort and reassurance; she cannot be expected to handle the direct, challenging feedback she might need in a stronger state.

Physicians, clergy, and every other caretaking, healing profession have the burden of being profoundly touched yet required to maintain a boundary around the extent and manner in which they act on that response. That's the separation. We may love and wish to nurture a client but must harness that impulse in ways appropriate to that client, in that relationship, and nothing more. The natural and healthy self-serving aspect of a normal human relationship is what is off the table for us, but the emotions and drives are simply part of being human. As a mother, I may have provided milk, cookies, and a hug, but therapists cannot do likewise.

The myth of compartmentalization flips to the other side as the therapist may use the illusory division of personal vs. public persona to justify actions that undercut the ethical expectations of a therapist. The same can be said of other professions, but, as a psychotherapist, I am comfortable using that very often misunderstood and misrepresented profession for this purpose.

Physician, heal thyself, and then leave yourself out of it. One of the interesting dilemmas of the mythical division of personal and professional, is that many people want to have it both ways. Professionals want it both ways, and the public wants it both ways, in very particular circumstances.

On the one hand, addicts famously assert that they can only be helped by other addicts because only someone with the disease of addiction, preferably the same variety, can really understand how they feel. From this position, the reach is made across the

That's My Personal Life

imaginary divide to therapists who are willing to be public with their diagnosis of addiction, and their status of being in recovery (from addiction). Because the majority-held current position in American psychiatry is that addiction is life-long disease, all sufferers are either actively using or in recovery. The fluidity of the disease and the supposed necessity of understanding from a fellow victim/patient requires a seamless flow between personal and professional. While other therapists are warned to avoid dual relationships except when utterly inescapable, addicts in the therapy field are overtly fellow sojourners in recovery with clients. That's not to say that therapists who are recovering addicts share every nuance of the journey with clients; some may, some may not. The difference is that the shared experience is a shortcut of sorts. Assured that the therapist who is also an addict will understand, an instant degree of trust is established. Unfortunately, the assumption of understanding sometimes extends to expecting more compassion when backsliding occurs; an addict knows what it's like to fall off the wagon and, in theory, would be more compassionate about the slip.

Addictions are not the only such example. It is perhaps the most common and, given the specialty certification available for addictions specialists in many states, it seems in this area, the link between personal experience and capacity to treat is generally accepted by practitioners, regulators and clients. Still, other problems or life experiences often matter to clients. Long-married clients seeking marriage counseling seem assured when they learn I have a 30+ years old union; parents struggling with behavior issues feel another parent will be less judging and more understanding. People of faith fear a non-religious therapist will be dismissive of the role of faith in their lives. This is not an unrealistic fear, of course; far more people outside of the mental health field value religion and spirituality than within it, where it is not too difficult to be labeled with "excessive religiosity." On the other hand, beginning in 1994, the Diagnostic and Statistical Manual of Mental Disorders began including a category for religious and spiritual problems,

Toxic Mythology

and there has been an influx of research on mental health and religion. Still, stereotypes remain:

> "Joseph," now deceased, was ordained clergy. He was a hospital chaplain in one hospital, and being treated for invasive cancer at another. He consulted me for guidance on how to interpret the psychologist's notes on his "excessive religiosity." Wearing his clerical garb, and invoking the importance of prayer were deemed excessive by the psychologist affiliated with the oncology program, as if he were delusional and wearing a costume. His trust in the hospital itself was affected, as he felt as if his strengths were devalued and wondered in what other ways he was being chronically misunderstood and even labeled as pathological.

On the other hand, most clients do not want to pay for therapy that turns into a session that is "all about" the therapist. The fine line between authenticity and appropriate here-and-now disclosure with a client, and divulging too much, is a wide gray field, and many ethical and experienced therapists will disagree on where to draw that line in every circumstance.

Clients also do not want a therapist who is, as some have proffered, "As messed up as [the client]." Cardiac patients are not comforted by seeing their cardiologist smoking in the hospital parking lot (as a friend has disclosed); therapy clients are certainly not uplifted by seeing their therapist performing an amateur, drunken flash dance on Saturday night (as shared with me by the unnamed client's subsequent therapist).

When it comes to personal vs. professional ethics, is it fair to ask any of us to choose? The domain of ethics and morality is one in which the myth of compartmentalization is increasingly being imposed on American citizens. Increasingly, both laws and professions' codes of ethics demand adherence to certain practices without regard to the professional's particular religious, moral or ethical stance. Lack of compliance is either a violation of law or a failure in professional ethics.

A few examples will illustrate:

That's My Personal Life

> Sweet Cakes by Melissa, an Oregon bakery, has been closed subsequent to legal investigations and a suit filed by a lesbian couple after the owners refused to bake a wedding cake for the same-sex nuptials, citing religious beliefs. The law requiring non-discrimination in accommodations in Oregon has no option to protect professionals from being forced to operate outside of their value systems.

The issue at hand is not whether GLBT persons have a right to marry or have cakes. That is the straw man set up by the media and certain factions in the government. The issue is whether a particular baker must bake a cake for an event that is in violation of that baker's religious beliefs. The laws of Oregon state, yes, the baker is either a baker for any and all potential paying clientele or the baker must be no baker at all. In the case cited, Reason magazine's reporter observed that attempts were made to entrap the baker by asking them to make cakes for other events that were, per the entrappers, also against Christian beliefs. An example given was human stem cell research, which reveals the ignorance of the anti-Christians involved. Plenty of Christians support stem-cell research; the Roman Catholic Church is invested in a company doing adult stem-cell research. It is embryonic stem cell research that is anathema for Christians. The point, however, is not the ignorance of the persecutors but the apparent assumption: a professional has no right to ever refuse to provide services. By extension, the Jewish therapist must accept the Nazi client, the Catholic African-American marriage counselor must work with the KKK couple, and the psychologist who is a member of PETA must serve the NRA member who comes to therapy in camouflage on the way to a weekend hunt.

> The American Psychological Association has asserted that their members in the U.S. military have the right to refuse to cooperate with orders that are possibly in opposition to the APA's Code of Ethics. The APA does not assert members' rights to refuse actions based on religious beliefs. Thus, if the military psychologist refuses to be engaged in interrogations due to the APA's stance on ethical treatment of prisoners, the APA will support her. If the same military

> *psychologist refers a same-sex couple to a colleague for counseling, because of the military psychologist's religious beliefs against same-sex relationships, the APA would consider this not within the psychologist's rights. In short, the APA holds its code of ethics in higher accord than religious codes.*

Here we see the arrogance of professional organizations in reference to their codes of ethics: a professional code surpasses religious codes. A faction within the American Medical Association has long asserted, for example, that any physician who refuses (for moral/religious reasons) to perform any legal medical procedure which she or he is capable of performing ought to stripped of the medical license and right to practice medicine. This would mean that a Catholic ob/gyn who respectfully refers a patient seeking an abortion to the colleague down the hall should be booted out of medical practice. The argument is that business is business, and personal beliefs have nothing to do with it. A child can see through the contradiction, as we will see below.

The effects on the public from such struggles within the various professions may not seem immediately clear. There is a trickle-down, and the trickle can seep far down.

Let us take the issue of the physician forced by law to participate in medical procedures she considers morally wrong. We see, then, that this physician will throw God under the bus. I cannot say I want to trust, with my very life, someone who will ignore God as she understands Him. I wonder what other expectations might be inconvenient in the moment, and result in a bad outcome for me. Will Hippocrates get a higher ranking than God? What about the most recent committee appointed for the American Medical Association Code of Ethics? What higher power will drive this physician to do what is right?

Taking it, perhaps, closer to home, how would you feel about a classroom teacher who would do what she considers immoral because the law says so? When there is an artificial delineation made between the private and public domains, the preferences of the powerful outweigh the understandings of the underlings.

> Children are coerced into participating in activities that are uncomfortable and, for some, downright harmful. Recently, an elementary school in Florida held an antibullying program in which children were ordered to say mean things to a dummy to see what it felt like to be a bully. Then the adult would rebuke them to demonstrate how bullying should be handled. Some children, no doubt all too familiar with being on the receiving end of cruel behavior, were reluctant to participate and quite distressed. It is against their principles to say mean things, especially without provocation, because someone told them to; yet an adult put them in this position and then criticized that very behavior. At the least it was confusing; moreover, it was a pint-sized introduction to the adult dilemma of being expected—nay, legally demanded—to behave in ways outside one's moral code right in public.

Another version of the compartmentalization myth is that we all exist in a fishbowl: the advent of social media has rendered all pretense at separation of public and private life merely a formality. In an electronic world, we are constantly monitored. Random comments that may have been tossed out as an aside at the water cooler are tweeted for followers. Pictures that would have been developed at the local shop, received with excitement and reviewed with a mix of glee (remember how much fun we had!) and disappointment (I had no idea that outfit looked like that; why didn't you tell me?) are now instantly posted online and the appalling habit of taking one's own photo in fisheye fashion—the "selfie" - was the word of the year for 2013.

The end result is the illusion that all is public, and deemed worth making public. People reluctant to constantly update their online "status" ("in the loo," "still in bed," etc.) may as well be troglodytes. The buffer between public and private is seen as a relic, some sort of bourgeois hangover. The trend continues from the electronic world into the material world.

Suffering under the delusion that it's foolish artifice to create such limitations, there has been a movement to remove any sense of propriety in public behavior. We are years into college women wearing pajamas and beachwear to classes while demanding their male counterparts treat them with solemn respect; young men, for their part, find it difficult to keep their pants on without a strange grip on their crotch. It may seem as if half the freshman class forgot to dress, and the other half are large four year olds in desperate need of a potty break. Youth, of course, specialize in pushing boundaries and are thus a poor example. There are others.

An extreme version is the movement in some circles towards owners' suites in which there is no privacy around the bathroom. The trend began in high-priced hotels and then, naturally, became the thing to do with the design-forward clique. Using the toilet in front of one's spouse is just one more thing to share. The illusion that intimacy equals lack of privacy is a dangerous one. It sounds like emotional abuse: if you love me, you'll tell me everything. If you really loved me, you would . . . use the toilet in front of me, too.

To go further and assert immodesty is merely modernity means that we are tearing aside any veils that separate humans from animals. This might be a disservice to animals: after all, cats dislike defecating in front of other cats, which is why the guidance on the ratio of cat litter boxes to cat in a home is one box per cat plus one extra box. Thus Fluffy need never do her business under the scornful eye Miss Kitty—although cat owners well know that cats will torment one another by refusing to leave, creating a miserable feline face-off just inches away from the possibility of relief. Cats, who clean their bottoms with their tongues, still know that some activities merit privacy.

A healthy, integrated life would balance between compartmentalization and the glass house. It would mean being ourselves: why is it so hard to do something as simple as merely being ourselves?

We are afraid. We are confused. We are burdened with our own, and others', expectations. Many wise people have written about this topic, and it requires more space than can be provided here. The essence, though, is that fear and apathy, those evil opposites of love and compassion, interfere with living an integrated life.

The integrated person's life reflects his values, at least most of the time, and when there is a mismatch, he or she deliberately seeks to make changes that create congruency between interior values and external actions. An integrated life means that when we are angry, we acknowledge our anger, seek to understand it, and use that information to make changes where needed. The integrated person may suffer, because emotions don't always comply with morals: the choice would be to yield to the passing emotional itch and compromise integrity, or be dishonest with oneself. The integrated person might have to decline certain invitations because the activity (a violent movie, a strip club, gambling) is counter to the person's values. This creates tension: others may question you, get defensive and from that position become offensive. *What's the matter with you? Can't you lighten up and have any fun? Oh, you think we're a bunch of losers/degenerates?* It can seem, at first glance, easier to dissemble or go along to get along. In the short term, it works in terms of deflecting criticism and postponing dealing with the challenge of living an integrated life. In the long term, it's just cross-contamination to be cleaned up before authenticity feels like a good fit.

Exhibitionism isn't the same as integration; after all, what is exhibitionism but an over-investment in being seen, being an experience for someone else? The exhibitionist objectifies herself and objectifies the observer; the observer, at least, is only objectifying one member of the transaction. Thus the person posting things on Facebook that prior generations would think shameful isn't being an integrated person so much as a mere exhibitionist who cannot be "me" without an audience. The integrated person needs no audience; the audience is immaterial. The values driving the behavior are the same; details of behavior may differ, but the essence remains unchanged. The person is congruent, or, as our grandparents might say, what you see is what you get.

THE ANTIDOTES:

Carl Rogers, one of the foundational figures of psychotherapy, postulated that three factors were essential for healing and growth in therapy: unconditional positive regard, congruency, and empathic understanding. The antidotes to the myth of compartmentalization can be summarized within the therapeutic factor, congruency.

Congruency of personhood is honesty: no masks, no putting on airs. While we might use tact to offer feedback to one another, the congruent person does not dissemble. In therapy, we are being honest even when tactful or using professional judgment to censor our feedback to provide what is necessary at that moment. Being congruent offers a sense of safety within the relationship and models what is often a novel type of behavior for clients. In the same way, congruency in all our relationships puts others at ease and allows us to live without juggling masks or trying to remember which story is "on" at the moment.

To enhance congruency:

Limit your time, and your child's time, in the virtual world.

This antidote turns up often in regard to the toxic myths, for good reason. The essence of much of modern technology is a self-congratulatory, artificial view of life. It is also often a life in third-person; experiences are recorded and reviewed later, rather than actively lived. The feedback of others in terms of comments or likes/dislikes become the barometer for the quality of an experience, or the distillation of that experience into a public exposition. Virtual-world enthusiasts run the risk of always being an outside assessor of their lives as they lived; it is impossible to fully live and simultaneously be an outside observer, rating experiences and in turn imagining those experiences as projections for others' consideration. Detachment from the virtual world may cause actual withdrawal symptoms, but ultimately will offer more peace and more authentic living.

Search for your authentic beliefs, and practice living as integrated a life as possible.

If we profess a particular faith, but don't live it, either we don't really believe it, or we are living incongruently, fearful of the cost of truly living in harmony with the belief system. The interaction between the hobo and the main character in the film, and book, "The Polar Express," presents this dilemma beautifully: who wants to be tricked into believing in a fairy tale? Believing in Santa, or Jesus, or any other belief system, demands we fall in line. "These people honor me with their lips, but their hearts are far from me (Matthew, 15:8)." No one's efforts will be perfect, but the attempt, and reflections on successes and failures in the attempt to live by our beliefs, is part of the foundation of spiritual and psychological growth.

When I worked with youth in religious education and parochial schools, I often told them, "If you are really Catholic, I will be able to tell it by watching you on the soccer fields, by seeing how you treat strangers in the grocery store or the mall, by watching you with your parents." Some children understood immediately, while a few others, more concrete in their thinking, wondered if they were supposed to walking around praying in public all the time. We had to address this specifically, given the developmental age of the children.

It may not be faith; it may be a need to integrate the assertion that "my family comes first," or, "my work ethic is important to me." In either case, if most actions don't bear it out, it is not authentic or not appropriately integrated into life.

Refer to your beliefs, morals and ethics in routine discussions of the day's events, current events, or the context of movies, theatre, music and literature.

Faith in the myth of compartmentalization leads to strange behaviors.

Toxic Mythology

> *Sarah has been highly involved in her synagogue for many years. From part-time employment to many roles as a volunteer, she is a familiar face to most members of the congregation. Now retired, Sarah has added a new column to her life besides volunteering and frequent attendance at worship: she has become addicted to very dark, violent television shows. She sees no apparent dilemma in bouncing her conversations with friends and family from difficulties in engaging older members into modernization efforts to an enthusiastic description of torture from a television drama. Her friends worry that Sarah may be deteriorating psychologically. They can see no other reasonable explanation for her holding these disparate interests.*

The myth of compartmentalization asserts that we can keep things separate. Why can't someone who prays in front of an abortion clinic because they assert a profound belief in the sanctity of human life feed an addiction to fictional characters who find creative ways to torture helpless people? Who are we to judge? Why can't a good person enjoy a little gore and violence now and then? The simple answer is that even if the myth sounds practicable on paper, it denies the reality of the human psyche. We are not designed to keep our mental parts in separate storage containers. There will be cross-contamination. The young men who access internet pornography, which is rapidly becoming more violent and debased, have difficulty seeing living, breathing women as fully human: ask their girlfriends, sisters, mothers, and professional contacts. A soldier with PTSD, who is successful in locking up the pain of combat, will ultimately either fail, with the pain leaking out in some other area of life, or will inadvertently lock up the capacity for love, connection, trust and warmth along with the anger, regret, fear and pain. We cannot, alas, have it both ways.

Let your value system step into your recreation. If you believe that violence is wrong except as a last resort to protect the innocent—the self-defense and just war position—then eschew violent movies and say why when asked (you will be). If you believe that the behavior of many professional athletes is shameful and you prefer not to support that by watching their games and buying their gear, then say so. When you wear the jersey, you are underwriting and condoning the behaviors on and off the field. Recreation is a good way for a family to develop congruence together, practice the language of congruence rather than compartmentalization, and develop confidence in resisting the myth of compartmentalization. When the family doesn't watch movies with unnecessary violence, because they believe in the sanctity of the human person/don't want to lose perspective on how terrible violence is/etc., the adults are providing the children with the mental scaffolding to organize a cohesive relationship between values and actions. Without the scaffolding, the default mode of the myth of compartmentalization becomes a steeper slippery slope.

7

Sticks and Stones

"STICKS AND STONES MAY break my bones, but names will never hurt me." So goes the childhood chant. It sounds brave and resilient, but it is also a clarion call for bullies to kick it up a notch and see about that bone-breaking business. The myth has, in many ways, been undercut by the focus in recent years on the unrelenting emotional battering produced through cyberbullying. Many people are justifiably concerned about the damage caused by cyber-bullying, revenge-porn, and harassment via various social media; others wonder if the current generation is being raised to be overly sensitive to anything disagreeable. While the handwringing over how, and whether, to protect children from bullying or let them learn to handle it themselves plays out, a large segment of popular culture glorifies the harassment of celebrities and feeds on a stream of gossip. Like so many modern toxic myths, the "sticks and stones" myth pleads to be taken both ways: it revels in the exploitation and humiliation of others, and asserts the victims ought not to be affected by the abuse and the schadenfreude of supposedly good people.

As with most interpersonal issues, the problem needs to be very carefully defined. Words mean different things to different people. A passing, teasing comment is not the same as bullying. Gentle and private correction is not the same as a public, humiliating put-down. Repeated, mean-spirited words create damage; these are bullying and abuse. Mistreatment has varied effects, depending on the age, emotional maturity and past experiences of the victim as well as the particular circumstances of the abuse.

As infants, we begin to learn about the world via our very first interactions. If the faces, hands and voices that attend to us are tender, gentle and respond quickly to our needs, we begin to build a mental scaffolding of the world as ultimately a safe and good place. This rudimentary skeleton of impressions is the starting point for the complex system of assumptions, expectations, and concepts that help form a unique personality. This child is, in a sense, inoculated to resist despair when disappointed. The sense of safety leads to a sense of budding competence. A child whose parents are usually quick to respond and attentive can be gently taught to calm herself, safe in knowing that if it is real distress, the adults will come and provide comfort. The child develops both confidence (I can handle this) and a sense of safety (if I need help, someone will help me). If, on the other hand, the infant's caregivers are frequently distracted, neglectful, cruel, or indifferent, the mental scaffolding will be the skeleton frame of mistrust, worry and fearfulness. The infant too young to self-soothe who is left to cry himself to sleep because the grownups erroneously believe comforting an infant less than 8 months old will "spoil" him, is indeed at risk of being "spoiled" in the sense of ruining the best opportunity to build a safe, secure sense of self and the world.

Through the preschool years, the child continues building the world view and sense of self. Humiliation, harsh punishment, and indifference can foster a sense of self that comprises shame, inadequacy and isolation. The child cannot trust herself or others. The normal mistakes of early childhood, from potty-training accidents to spilled milk, are interpreted as evidence of being a failure. Later, when the social challenges of elementary school arise, this child is likely to absorb the blame for others' cruelty. She believes she deserves it, or caused it by her own inadequacy. She is unlikely

Toxic Mythology

to report the mistreatment. Experience has indicated that no one cares, anyway.

Even children blessed with loving grownups and a secure early childhood easily succumb to devastation when verbally abused and bullied by peers. This is especially so during adolescence, a stage which begins earlier than ever, and on the other end, seems to continue until 10 years or more into legal adulthood. There are a few factors involved in adolescents' susceptibility to bullying.

Adolescents are supposed to segue from complete dependence and identification with their family of origin to an individual sense of self. Along the way, peers become increasingly important as a type of psychological mirror. The approbation of peers replaces the approval of parents as a gauge of worthiness. This hunger for peer acceptance is a potentially dangerous Achilles' heel for adolescents, and is exacerbated by the so-called "spotlight effect," an aspect of adolescent psychological development in which they believe everyone notices everything they're doing, that the social spotlight is on them. Every wrong answer in class, every spot of acne, every hair out of place seems blaringly obvious to the teen and, he supposes, to everyone else.

During adolescence, the brain reworks vital connections between emotion and reason. The child who seemed sensible at 12 can seem, and often be, irrational at 15. Hormonal rushes feed the increased impulsivity that is a side-effect of a process of maturation. The brain is rewiring and, in the meantime, is less efficient in terms of reason. Without adequate braking from the logical part of the brain, emotions become tyrannical replacements for thinking. Emotions don't think about the future; emotions live in the now of physiological arousal. It is extremely hard for adolescents to back away from strong emotions and put things in perspective.

Any effort to consider other points of view is complicated by teens' erroneous belief that only people their own age can understand them. They resist input from older people, whom they see as not being able to identify with the experiences and emotions they experience. The girl who turned trustingly to her mother with all her fears and secrets at 10 may be screaming at that same mother that, "You can't understand! You never understand! You don't know what it's like!" when the mother attempts to discuss the child's latest social feud a few years later.

The common dependence on electronic social media makes this worse. Terrified of missing something, including missing the opportunity to respond to cruelty or criticism, adolescents and many adults struggle to extricate from cyberspace even for a few hours of sleep. Teenagers take their phones to bed and respond to text messages throughout the night, disrupting their sleep and creating more problems due to sleep deprivation. Cyberspace makes bullying a potentially constant feature of life.

> Kayla, age 14, has been friends with Alicia and Jasmine since kindergarten. Inseparable through 7th grade, something has changed this school year. Alicia and Jasmine seem to be spending time together without Kayla, and Kayla's desperate attempts to stay with them in class, in the halls, and at lunch are met with evasiveness and conversations about things that don't involve Kayla. It escalates to outright verbal rudeness, and then to text messages berating Kayla, asking her why she can't get a life, leave them alone, stop being a loser, etc. Pictures are posted on line of Kayla in unremarkable but now embarrassing situations: asleep with a stuffed animal at a slumber party, taken three years ago; in a cute but now humiliating Halloween costume taken 2 years ago. Kayla doesn't tell her parents what's going on; she tries to get out of going to school and begins suffering somatic symptoms. Her parents know something is wrong but their attempts to talk to Kayla meet with resistance, slammed doors, accusations of trying to run her life and complaints about their inability to understand. After months of being bullied, in person and in cyberspace, Kayla overdoses on over-the-counter cold medications and nearly dies. A few weeks later, in the family therapist's office, Kayla is still wondering what she did wrong to make her friends so mad at her.

Adults find it frustrating that children react so powerfully to the rejection of peers. Why can't they see that this is just temporary, that next month or next year, this really won't be as terrible as it seems right now? It is hard to remember, as adults, what it was like to be a child. Adults imagine ourselves as children but often impose our grown-up self into a memory that was experienced by someone smaller, frailer, less intellectually advanced, helpless, and existentially at risk. Thus the victim of childhood sexual abuse blames herself for not fighting back because the adult she has become is bigger, stronger, and knows resisting might work. The four-year-old child she was at the time weighed 30 pounds and was utterly helpless, paralyzed by fear and confusion. In the same way, we recall childhood humiliations and imagine all sorts of things we could have done, except, of course, we could not, because we had not the maturity, insight or other resources to do so. We are putting a heroic mature self into that old film to write a new ending, and while there is a certain useful narrative therapeutic process in that, it is not useful when it only leads to abusing oneself with blame and guilt. In some ways, the adult survivor of childhood abuse, whether physical, emotional or sexual, easily becomes an echo reinforcing the abuse by blaming the past-self for failing to put up an adult's fight.

Not all adults develop the maturity to be even a little resistant to the "sticks and stones" of verbal cruelty. The lingering effects of early neglect or mistreatment include a shaky sense of self. Every stage of development subsequent to that mistreatment may be resting on an inadequate, inaccurate foundation. The shamed, harshly punished toddler who internalizes, "I am bad and no one likes me," goes on to frame self-as-student, self-as-friend, and self-as-life-partner as someone who is deeply flawed and unlovable. Challenging that foundational belief and building a new, healthier perspective on the self is possible. It will require a lot of work. The "A-ha!" moment of realization may come as a spiritual experience, or a philosophical insight. That's the quick part. Next comes a long span of rehearsing the new way of thinking, and learning to filter life's experiences through the novel route, as the brain develops new connections to re-organize memories and frame new experiences through the lens of being a worthwhile person.

Sticks and Stones

Self-worth, from the earliest stages of life, is a powerful anchoring heuristic. We all have anchoring heuristics; they are particular mental shortcuts and belief systems which are our "default" modes. Imagine, for example, a person who has been blessed with a secure, loving environment. One of her anchoring heuristics is that most people are basically good. She may run into some mean people, and feel a little discouraged, angry, or fearful; but that anchoring belief soon pulls her back. The disappointments don't push her off her center. Conversely, the child who has an insecure sense of the world will run into nice people, but may be skeptical, believing they're really not nice, or believe that the people will only be nice until they, "find out what I'm really like." The anchoring heuristic of unworthiness colors every interaction and builds a festering sense of hopelessness. When cruelty is encountered, it seems almost inevitable.

Early life experiences are not the only reason someone may be extremely vulnerable to verbal cruelty. Substance abuse can create a kind of arrested development. Maturation is an inherently painful process, and drugs dull the pain and thus interfere with full integration of the personality. The forty-year-old alcoholic may be emotionally fifteen but look like a haggard fifty-year-old, flailing in search of respect and seeking approval from what is probably a shrinking pool of comrades.

This leaves healthy adults: what of them? It's a good thought, that one can be resilient and resist buying into verbal abuse and cruel messages. We can develop immunity. Without this sort of emotional "vaccine," adult life can become chronically painful. There doesn't have to be overt cruelty; small, nagging negativity and the fear of being left out create misery:

> Margi started working in the bookkeeping department of a mid-size corporation with six other women two years ago. Most of them have worked together for ten years. They joke amongst themselves, share joys and concerns, and complain about one another's quirks. There is a certain amount of negative gossip. Margi claims to like her job and coworkers, but she suffers chronic headaches, stomach

> upset and mild anxiety. She worries during vacations, ruminating on her fears that her colleagues are using her absence to complain about her as they do about others. She is usually nearly distraught by the time she returns to her job. The same anxiety about disapproval leads to difficulty dressing for work, selecting birthday cards for her coworkers, and trying to balance her fear of ostracism with her desire to avoid participating in the gossip she fears.

Margi has invested a lot into her job and the approval of her peers. Rather than enjoying their acquaintanceship, she has elevated their friendship to a need. Gradually, her mental energies have focused on her work and office politics rather than finding a balance between work and home. As her emotional life becomes more enmeshed with work, the approval of colleagues begins to outweigh the apparent importance of the approval and love of family and friends. The fear of criticism infects her, leading to worry when away from the office about what is being said about her, panicked paralysis about dressing for work for fear of a disapproving eyebrow raise, and subsequently she cramps her emotional life to fit into a cubicle.

Not all adults who fear disapproval are in Margi's relatively enviable position. Some forms of disapproval and criticism are much more threatening and real. In such cases, inoculation is not enough. Words can damage reputations and careers, even when there has been no wrongdoing, and the victim may be helpless to address the problem. My clinical experience with this follows; the example is a hybrid of several situations:

> Mark suffers with a debilitating level of anxiety. The symptoms are physical and psychological: his racing heart and surging adrenaline are accompanied by persistent thoughts that focus on his faults, real and imagined. Solid research indicates that an approach that includes training in a specific mindfulness process plus cognitive-behavioral therapy will probably be most helpful, based on the considerable research by Dr. Jeffrey Schwartz, among others. By learning to slow down and focus on his five senses as a mindfulness process, Mark will be able to train his mind to stay in the

present; then with cognitive-behavioral counseling, he will be able to counter the now automatic self-critical thoughts and replace them. When I discussed these approaches with Mark, he accepted the recommendations. However, before his next appointment, he emailed to let me know he would not be returning. A devout Christian, his internet research led him on a path from the specific mindfulness practice I recommended to various New Age practices. He decided this meant I was recommending something against his religious beliefs, consulted a clergyman, who recommended Mark not participate in this. My effort at educating him in the difference between psychological mindfulness practices of here-and-now awareness versus the practices he feared would be a violation of his religion was not fruitful. I have no way to counter whatever damage may be done to my reputation; even if I knew which of the many clergy in the area he had contacted. I could not clarify my research-based, religion-friendly recommendation. I am bound to protect Mark's privacy in ways he need not protect mine. In this case, words may have indeed hurt me.

Misunderstandings and gossip are words that do hurt, perhaps in complicated and reputation-damaging ways.

THE ANTIDOTES:

As I've discussed, the myth has two faces. It is, in some ways, true: to some extent, mature and healthy people can be well-inoculated from the potential damage of most verbal attacks. On the other hand, children, vulnerable adults and professional reputations are all at risk of deep, irreversible damage from others' words.

Begin at the beginning . . . or begin right now, to create a safe environment that encourages security, trust, and confidence.

Building a healthy scaffolding for psychological development begins before we are born, with good nutrition and a safe, calm mother whose bloodstream is not surging with adrenaline. If you, or the children in your care, didn't have that benefit, you can begin immediately to create a healthy sense of self and an overall sense of security in close relationships.

> Diana came to live with her aunt and uncle, Lisa and Ben, at age 6. By that time, she'd been in foster care on and off for three years as her mother repeatedly lost custody of Diana due to drug abuse and arrests for possession, prostitution, and theft. Diana was secretive, stealing small items from the general living quarters, including food, and hiding these things in her room. She lied about her behavior, hid reports from school, and was often defiant. Struggling to fit in at school, she alternated between being quarrelsome and withdrawn with teachers; she was intrusive and needy with the other children. Her behaviors pointed clearly to the deep insecurity she felt her entire life. At 6, she was unable to articulate her deep fears of being rejected and her fear of not having what she needs to live. Lisa and Ben focused on safety and security first. They made sure home was as predictable and steady as possible, with regular routines. They patiently modeled using words, not actions, to express feelings and helped Diana by providing feeling words when she struggled to articulate her anguish at being rejected during recess or reprimanded in class. They provided consequences that were predictable, given calmly and which fit the offense, without raising their voices. Lisa and Ben praised Diana's efforts, and let family and friends know how well Diana was doing at home and at school.

Diana's experiences with Lisa and Ben are providing a second chance to build healthy mental scaffolding. As she learns the world can be predictable and safe, and that even negative feelings can be accepted by loved ones, she will become confident in herself and willing to turn to her new family when problems arise in other environments.

We can help one another express emotions with safety. Clinical experience teaches me that many adults have difficulty separating thoughts, emotions and behaviors. They become fearful of their own emotions because they cannot differentiate the emotion from the associated action. Thus, they squelch the emotions, feel ashamed, and are even more vulnerable to distress from criticism and other verbal attacks. Anger is just an emotion; it can be quite useful. It is a combination of psychological and physical sensations, usually arising from recognizing an unmet need or desire. One version of anger may be the hurt we feel when coworkers go out for lunch without inviting us along. Sitting down with our own lunch and a good book is a smart, useful way to use the energy of anger. Another version may be the helpless, silent rage of overhearing someone we trusted repeat a story told in confidence. Confronting the action may or may not be useful; using the emotion to guide a decision on being a better judge of character is another option. Having someone who will listen and not be critical of the emotions is important. You don't need to approve of the actions someone has chosen to use to express that emotion to create a safe emotional environment. You can express empathy for the child who is angry about being taunted while still holding the child accountable for the naughty behavior chosen to express that anger.

Part of the safe environment for emotional expression—for sharing the hurts and disappointments that others inflict - can include questions. Avoid "why" questions; "why" triggers defensiveness; it seems to imply criticism. Instead, provide feedback that shows interest and an attempt to understand deeply. It may take practice.

> *Bobby, age 11, came home from school visibly upset. Every step echoed angrily; usually "starving," he tried to bypass the kitchen and retreat to his room. Coaxing him into the kitchen for a snack, Mom was eventually able to draw out a little of what happened.*
>
> *"I just hate PE, that's all," Bobby announced. "Why do we have to have that stupid class? We never do anything anyway. I don't know why we even have to change; it's not like we're getting messy. Besides, the locker room stinks." It didn't take genius to infer the problem involves the locker room, and probably Bobby's nemesis, his former-best-friend, Alan.*

Toxic Mythology

> "Yeah, you seem pretty aggravated about it," was all Mom said. Note that she's not criticizing his language ("hating") or giving him a list of rationale for physical education. She's not correcting his mistaken impression that he doesn't smell bad after exercising. She does sound compassionate and offers him a feeling word—aggravated—to help him with his rumbling emotions.
>
> "I don't know about aggravated. I just . . . I mean . . . well, it would be better if stupid Alan wasn't in my class. He just . . . he ruins everything."
>
> Mom nods to herself. Yes, it's Alan again. She offers, "It must be really frustrating to be stuck in PE with Alan. Last semester you were able to have fun in that class but this semester it's just been so hard to deal with him."
>
> "You know what happened today? Today . . . "

Bobby's mom has created an environment where Bobby's emotions are accepted. Later, when he confesses to having punched Alan after Alan showed everyone the text he'd just sent to a girl Bobby likes, telling her about Bobby's style of underpants, she'll have to balance compassion for the feelings with compassion for Bobby's having to go to in-school suspension on Saturday. Bobby will have consequences for his actions, and he will also know that even though his parents will enforce the consequences, they understand his feelings. The parents may secretly believe Bobby's behavior was entirely justified and may reasonably consult with the school personnel to be sure that Alan is also being held accountable for cyber-bullying. Alan's use of words and photographs to humiliate and shame Bobby did hurt. Telling Bobby not to care about what Alan says, or does, denies the reality of the hurt caused by public humiliation for anyone, particularly a young adolescent whose fear of public disapproval is amplified beyond the level of either childhood or adulthood. In short, provide one another with the ability to express emotions with safety. Differentiate between the feelings (sad/angry/etc.) and the behaviors, and validate one another's feelings without buying into the rationale and actions.

Know what you're experiencing and deal with the reality of the situation.

The world moves very quickly, and the unrelenting noise of modern life is very effective at short-circuiting reflection. It is all too easy to be swept along, mistaking emotions for thoughts and impressions for reality. The similarity to the plot against humanity Screwtape describes to Wormwood in C.S. Lewis' *The Screwtape Letters* is unnerving. Screwtape, to remind readers, mentioned the use of popular media and lots of incessant noise to distract us from things that are good and wholesome. In Lewis' time, it was print media, radio and the first decade or so of television; our own media is even more pervasive and diverse. Overcome by lots of stimulation and endless entertainment, we are set up, then, to not really name what's happening. Gossip is damaging, to the speaker, the listener, and the victim.

> *Cheryl was laid off six months ago. Bored and lonely, she jokingly admits she is "addicted" to social media, spending a few hours a day updating her own status and checking in on her dozens of contacts, who comprise family, friends, and vague connections via those friends. Encouraged by approval in the online universe, her posts become increasingly revealing. She begins to post complaints about her husband and her teenaged children. Her friends commiserate. The posts become more detailed. Naturally a good storyteller, Cheryl's descriptions of her daughter's dramatics, her son's awkward skateboarding through adolescence and her husband's foibles are popular posts. Others pass them along. Cheryl doesn't stop to reflect on how these stories reflect on her family, or on her. When her daughter confronts her in a tearful rage, demanding to know why Mom has been telling "everyone" about her personal business, Cheryl is at a loss for words. A popular pastime, begun innocently, turned into a deep addiction to gossip as a means to gain attention and approval.*

Cheryl did not notice that she was spiraling down from lighthearted conversation into gossip. She was failing to reflect on her

Toxic Mythology

own actions, modeling poor behavior for her children, and seeking approval without considering the cost. Her daughter clearly feels as if the security of home has been breached; how her husband and son will react to having their lives peeled open for strangers' entertainment remains to be seen.

It's not surprising that Cheryl doesn't recognize gossip until confronted with the humiliation her actions has created. Much of what passes for news and entertainment is really just gossip. Overexposure leads to desensitization. Instead of pitying a politician whose trash was ransacked by reporters looking for dirty laundry, it's often relished by viewers, especially if the politician belongs to the "wrong" party. This teaches our children that certain differences dehumanize others. Limit exposure and accurately identify what is actually happening. Express compassion for the famous person and resist supporting the gossip industry.

Tend to your scaffolding.

At whatever stage you and others around you may be, pay attention to the scaffolding you are building. How you organize incoming information and link it to your values and knowledge will impact your capacity to resist the depth of damage verbal abuse can cause. Recall Margi, who was so dependent on coworkers' approval of her behavior and appearance that she found it difficult to prepare for work in the morning. By excessively valuing anyone's praise, rather than focusing on the praise of those whose opinions are truly important to her, she became vulnerable to depression and despair at the disapprobation of people not as significant to her long-term happiness. Striving for the praise and attention of relative strangers is a sign of deep insecurity. Is the world is so unpredictable and unsafe that even the indifferent nod of a stranger feels like a lifeline?

Imagine if Margi works to reduce her dependence on her coworkers' approval:

> Six months later, Margi is well into a program of silent self-improvement. Using a science-based self-help book on cognitive-behavioral therapy, she has been examining

and changing her automatic thoughts about herself and her coworkers. She realized that she's been insecure her entire life, and has been wasting a lot of energy seeking approval from people who really don't care about her. She has started investing more of that energy in to her "real" life outside of work. Her family life has improved and she's begun going for long walks with her husband during the time she's reclaimed by not panicking over her appearance before work every day. She took a week's vacation and occasionally worried about the piled-up work she'd have to do on her return. The thought about what was being said about her in her absence popped up a few times, but she was able to dismiss the worry and focus on fun.

As she continues this process, Margi will become increasingly less dependent on random approval and more resilient when the inevitable office politics sometimes leaves her out of the in-group.

Part of that scaffolding includes developing a long-term view. A long-term view is not possible for most people until adolescence, when the brain matures enough to allow abstract thinking. Developing a long term view, and the self-control to refocus on that view, are vital in putting daily disappointments in proper perspective. Impulse control is identified as a key trait of successful people for good reason. Adolescents, and those trapped in psychological adolescence, are unable to maintain an extended future focus. Ruled by the emotions of the moment and vulnerable to any glint of disapproval or rejection, the pain in the moment feels like it will be pain forever.

This can reinforce the feelings of hopelessness and worthlessness people often call depression. Sometimes it grows because of the cognitive error of reacting to an emotion as if the emotion were an accurate assessment of the situation. Maybe the emotion fits; maybe it doesn't fit. Maybe you are that distressed about your colleague's snide remark because you were already upset by an unexpectedly high utility bill, an argument about the thermostat with your spouse, and a call from your child's principal about yet another fight in the cafeteria. Overwhelmed with stress, your brain seeks to make sense of it. If your thoughts settle on the most recent annoyance, this time the rude coworker, your mind elevates that coworker to a more important status. After all, just an offhand criticism has sent you into the depths of despair. You are likely to be more sensitive to his rudeness until you make an effort to resist those thoughts and subsequent feelings.

Depression can also grow out of the cognitive error of seeing one negative event as an irrevocable step in an endless cycle of negative events. People who are resistant to despair and depression are able to view current difficulties as present challenges rather than predictive of the rest of life. Correct this error by challenging the seemingly automatic thoughts that rear up in the face of rejection or disappointment and replacing them with more realistic thoughts that are believable, not simplistic and shallow.

Words can be very damaging, but we have the resources to use words to build our immunity to verbal cruelty and abuse. Even those who were cheated out of a nurturing childhood can learn to minimize the damage words create.

8

Conclusion

THE MYTHS SEEM SO . . . OBVIOUS. Each chapter in this book has no doubt triggered at least one, "Well, everyone knows that," comment for readers. That's part of the danger implicit in these myths. On one hand, they seem self-evident: we all know that money doesn't really buy happiness, and we all know that words can, and do, hurt us. Yet it is plain to see that, self-evident as they may be, they are no more acted upon in that regard than the self-evident truths asserted by our founding fathers.

Familiarity breeds contempt. We have been exposed to the myths so often that most of us are unaware of the subtle pressures and slow poisoning they incur. Conquering the myths requires understanding human nature. Effecting true, deep change in ourselves challenges deeply held beliefs. Such changes are often briefly disorienting and require tenacity. When these myths are part of the fabric of your formative years, they become embedded in your underlying assumptions about the world. For many people, one or more of the toxic myths is so deeply engrained that it is part of the basic scaffolding on which much more obvious knowledge has been layered. Even if an "A-ha!" moment has been experienced, it is unlikely to lead to a profound change and an instantaneous

Toxic Mythology

shedding of unhealthy, unhappy assumptions about the world and oneself. While many people can identify a pivot point—a moment in time when they realized a deep awareness of the need for a major life change—the reality is that, pivot point or not, the change itself was arduous, often discouraging and unpleasant, and at times seemed doomed to failure. The change may require a daily recommitment, as those who belong to twelve-step programs will attest.

Take, for example, letting go of the myth that your opinion is as good as anyone else's. It can be a profound relief to give up the burden of having to have an opinion on anything and everything someone else may bring up in conversation, but it can be very difficult to accept that this means others may not accept your demurring on taking a stance. To fail to have an opinion seems like failing to have a mind, and yet, how much more accurate and honest to assert that one doesn't know enough about a topic to have an opinion. Refuting the myth means giving up a little bit of false pride and the defense that being able to take a position offers us.

Each of the myths has multiple facets. Like real myths, the toxic myths hold a bit of truth, but instead of being offered up as a way of delivering a greater truth, the toxic myths distort and corrupt real truths, leaving us with empty promises, faulty guidance and a mental structure seemingly designed to inflict misery on ourselves and others.

In many ways, the antidotes to these myths often overlap. As you have no doubt noticed, some themes come through many chapters:

Be aware of the choices you make, great and small, and describe them to yourself as choices.

Whether electing to sleep late, take a single serving at dinner, or "borrow" office supplies from your employer for your child's science project, you are making a choice. Be aware of it: own it, name it, and be honest with yourself about the choices you make. Likewise, offer and label choices as you see them made by the children in your care. Thank them for good choices (behaving well in the grocery store) and express regret about poor ones (deciding not to study for a test).

Selectively tune out of mainstream culture.

More than an hour or so of recreational screen time per day is not good for grownups, and is very bad for younger people, whose brains and minds are not ready to filter the incoming messages, discerning good from bad. Most adults have a difficult time of it, as experts have carefully modulated the messages to fly under the radar of our awareness. Even if you are painfully aware of the manipulations being attempted, the simple truth is that the brain processes repeated exposure to the same stimulus as separate, unique experiences. This is one reason that psychologists were concerned about the constant reviewing of the attacks on the World Trade Center: adults and children alike were being re-stimulated with the biochemical effects of horror and fear, reinforcing those emotions and the chemical effects as if the attacks had happened repeatedly. Indeed, for smaller children caught up in watching the endless coverage with their panicked adults, it truly did seem to happen repeatedly. Even if you are watching educational programming, the subtle messages (others your age have more stuff, are more attractive, seem happier) infect us quietly, leaving a vague restlessness and self-criticism, where we might otherwise have been satisfied and even grateful.

Connect with others often and deeply.

It is very easy to rush through our interactions without actually seeing other people. We look, but do not really see; we hear but do not really listen. The toxic myths promote separation, envy and alienation rather than connection and compassion. A simple interaction of greeting, done with full attention and warmth, will change things. More attention to the interaction means the other person will be elevated from some sort of environmental prop to an actual person, giving each of you a chance to recognize and honor one another's humanity. Feeling like a real person, not invisible or insignificant to others, is a powerful antidote to the toxic myths.

Live by your values, and regularly examine your life to see if your small choices really reflect those values or are undercutting your authenticity.

Would someone following you through a typical day be able to accurately identify your top priorities and most cherished beliefs? If your real values are not apparent from your daily routine and demeanor, then your life is not authentic.

Question common knowledge.

It often isn't common, and it often isn't knowledge. "Everyone knows," usually means a few people believe, or want desperately to believe, or want you to believe, some thinly veiled message (possibly even a marketing message) likely to lead to unhappiness. Being cynical isn't an antidote to the toxic myths, but being respectfully curious and questioning can be. Remember our bullied Tony? "Everyone" says you will get in terrible trouble for defending yourself, or that ignoring bullying will make it stop. Tony and his parents need to question that common knowledge, because it is probably neither. There are ways to defend oneself; sometimes "trouble" is relative; and ignoring bullying does not lead to the bully becoming bored and wandering off in pursuit of a more responsive target.

Respect language.

Use words accurately; don't imitate others' use of words without investigating. Bookmark an online dictionary and use it regularly; check to see if a word that stymies you actually fits in the place in which you find it. Be aware, too, of how you influence yourself

Conclusion

with the words you choose in your silent thoughts as well as spoken words. Entire, research-supported theories of psychological healing are based on the power of our words to create or amplify emotional states. Dramatic words amplify emotional responses to events, deserved or not; minimizing words belittle or scorn our responses to events. By the same token, we have to be willing to accept that others' use of words may be different than our own. When a client complains of feeling "depressed," for example, I cannot assume the particular emotional pain subsumed for that client within that term. So when people assert something is "cool" or "popular," or "essential" or "critical," we cannot assume they mean what we might mean, any more than we might concur that something is "obvious."

The antidotes to most of the myths are within the simple but often difficult rhythm of the moral, reflective pursuit of a deeply meaningful life.

It is simple because it is in many ways straightforward. It is difficult because the way forward can be arduous. It is like a marathon: the simple process of placing one foot in front of the other becomes a challenge when it must be repeated for 26.2 miles. And yet, completing this simple action of placing one foot in front of the other enough times will end in the successful completion of the race.

www.ingramcontent.com/pod-product-compliance
Lightning Source LLC
Chambersburg PA
CBHW070922160426
43193CB00011B/1555